I Was Knocked Down But Not Out!
How My Faith Got Me Through!
The Raw and Uncut Story

Derek G. Matthews

PAGE PUBLISHING, INC.
New York, NY

First originally published by Page Publishing, Inc. 2017

ISBN 978-1-63568-727-9 (Paperback)
ISBN 978-1-63568-728-6 (Digital)

Printed in the United States of America

This book is a raw compilation of writings, with very little edits, that I composed while going through a period of transition of my life in prison, and is intended to give the reader a snapshot of my life in various trials that I have faced. My next writings will reveal more of my life when the timing allows me to say things and not feel the need to protect myself and others from the things I choose not to say yet.

INTRODUCTION

$\mathcal{T}$OO MANY OF US SUFFER from what I may refer to as "purpose disease." In other words, they have reached a certain level or obtained a goal and decided that was their purpose. Now they are coasting through life off of what they have already learned. While in federal prison, I learned that nearly 50 percent of people, after they've graduated from high school, will never read an entire book the rest of their adult life. One reason is that people see learning as a period of life instead of a way of life. They think, *I'm out of school. I'm done with my training. I've got my big GS-15 job and corner office and I'm good.*

But God never created us to reach one level and stop. Whether you're 90 or 105 years old or 6 years old, you should be constantly learning, improving your skills, and getting better at what you do. The key is that you take responsibility for your own growth. Growth is not automatic. What steps are you taking? In this book, I will break down some I either did take and in some cases some I did not take. Are you reading books? Listening to CDs? Going to seminars? Do you have a mentor? How do you handle the feeling of being sick and tired? I want you to read this book and either begin to develop skills or enhance what you already do and not continue to coast through life relying on what you have already learned or even worse, "what you think you know."

You have a huge pot of gold inside of you. Let's develop your talent and become all that God has created you to be.

As I sat in in federal prison the first week and gathered my thoughts to determine what direction to go to in my writings, one night, I was led to the book of Ephesians. As we know, Paul writes his letter from prison (Ephesians 4:1 probably in Rome, Acts 28:30–31) to the church he started in Ephesians (Acts 19). In the first half, he explains God's great plan to redeem the world through Christ. Showing what this means for individual Christians and for the whole church. In the second half, he gives practical advice on how to live the Christian life. In the second half, he gives practical advice on how to live the Christian life. As I read the book, I had to begin to examine myself to be sure that I was really saved. Once I was sure after my gut check, I was and am still ready to stand tall to fight Satan and show my unconditional love to my family, my church, and my community.

I had a vision that several inmates and I were falling off a cliff in solitary confinement and were just in midair. We began to reach out and touch one another and join together. And I heard the Lord say, "My desire is for you, my children, to reach out, interact with each other, and join together on a spiritual level rather than just on a natural level."

"Now, therefore, you are no longer strangers and foreigners, but fellow citizens with the saints and members of the household of God, having been built on the foundation of the apostles and prophets, Jesus Christ Himself being the chief cornerstone, in whom the whole building, being fitted together, grows into a holy temple in the Lord, in whom you also are being built together for a dwelling place of God in the Spirit" (Ephesians 2:19–22).

I ran across an article that talked about how to reduce the risk of being laid off. There are three main things that employers look for when deciding who to keep. They want to keep people who are positive, people who are versatile, and people who are always improving. Ask yourself, "What are you?" Get yourself motivated!

Are you focused on developing your gifts in such a way that your company or government job you love so much cannot make it without you? Do they notice that things don't run nearly as smoothly when you are not there? If you take a week off and nobody misses you, all the work gets done and sales and production go just as good as if you were there. Unless you are the owner, it's time to sound your inner alarm and start moving in the right direction NOW. If you are not being missed, then maybe you are "not needed." You need to kick it into a new gear and start producing more than you have been until reading this book because time is either your best friend or your worst enemy because it waits for no one and you need to decide what it is for you.

Scripture is clear, when we sharpen our skills, when we work with a spirit of excellence. We will stand before great men. Leaders will begin to take notice, either in church, community, or your work. Promotions come. Like cream rising to the top, you will rise to greater heights as well. Remember to keep doing your best, as you stay faithful and keep growing. God will cause you to be noticed and move forward in the life blessing he has prepared for you.

Your Daily Prayer

Father, thank you for the gifts and talents you have given me. Help me see the areas where I can rise higher. I desire to serve diligently with an attitude of excellence so that I can bring you glory in everything that I do, in Jesus' name. Amen.

Purpose

This book was written to provide my perspective on how to overcome adversities in our lives by knowing that whatever battles you face, the world does not stop or even pause when you think what you are faced with is the end of the world. I want you to read this and learn to tell yourself you can be anything you allow your thoughts to say you can be, but you must understand that your sacrifice to get to that goal should make you cry when the fight is over. Tears of victory and not tears of defeat. The power of positive thinking and the power of faith and your ability to be humble enough to let God show you the way is what I want to expose you to. This is based on my story and my story alone, but you will note mine resembles many great men that came before me and you, and after reading, I'm sure you will find that yours is not much different than mine ... God bless you.

"Commit to the Lord whatever you do, and your plans will succeed" *(Proverbs 16:3)!*

DEDICATION

*T*HIS BOOK IS DEDICATED TO the memory of my loving mother, Rev. Callie M. Johnson-Matthews, who departed the earth on October 2, 2013, to go home to God after her second battle with cancer. She remains my voice of reason and the Why that makes me cry. To God be the glory. I love you, Mom.

Your Suga

SPECIAL DEDICATION

To my late brother Robert, Lil Brother, I miss you every day and pray that you are resting well in heaven with Mom and looking down on us. Our good times are what I keep close as I keep your memory going. Whenever someone says something about having a good time, I immediately think of you and what good times meant in your eyes. The two gifts you left us behind are both a bundle of your special joy, and, bro, I love you. I pray that those who read this story get a taste of how real this life is and enjoy what they can while they can, but most of all, they appreciate it as a gift from above.

Rest well, my brother.

ACKNOWLEDGMENTS

O MY LOVING WIFE, I thank you for being my ride-and-die and sticking through thick and thin, sickness and health. Many thanks to my two incredible children and your resilience through the storms and your continued love and respect for me as your father. Thanks to my Father for giving us life, and to my siblings, I want you all to know that I love you more than words can say, and I'm proud to call you my sisters and brother. Special thanks to my in-laws who are the best anyone could ask for. Thank you both for treating me like a son and a brother and being there, no matter what. Also many thanks to my church family and spiritual supporters and clergy. Last but surely not least, that group of core friends who stayed with our household from the beginning all the way through today without hesitation and ensured that no matter what, whether being called upon or volunteering your time to drive, pick-up, drop-off, or just plain assist, you did what needed to be done.

There are many others who prayed for me during the rough times, and I appreciate that very much.

I WAS BORN JUNE 11, 1966, to a young couple very much in love and freshly married. My mother was so proud of her firstborn child that she began documenting her new role as a mom with a photo album and notes with each photo through my entire childhood life and later up to my marriage and slightly after. This book will describe and explain my life as a young man and rise to being one of the most affluent African-American men in the country surrounding security and law enforcement training and operations to my experience in federal prison. Let the story be inspiring to you, but please understand that the intent is about making good and sound decisions and how important it is to not just know about God, yet it's better to really know him by having an intimate relationship with him, and if you don't have such a relationship, how quickly your life can change.

I don't expect this story to stop you from doing what you feel you must do, but give you a better understanding of the importance of listening to God when he speaks to you. I grew up in a small city called Annapolis, Maryland, in a "one way in-one way out" community where my parents lived in their first apartment and paid about $66 per month in rent. Both my parents were hard workers and focused on what they loved to do and knew best.

Let's start with my mother as I may refer to her at times as my GPS. She was the son of Pastor, so let's focus here for a moment. She had two siblings, an older brother Uncle Clarence and her sister and my Auntie Eloise, the one who gave me my middle name, yes, Greyland. These two girls had a mom and dad growing up who loved them and showed them a solid foundation. My mother was a public servant from birth until her passing. She worked as a teacher's aide in Lothian. (Remember Lothian because it will come back later.) She also worked at the YWCA. (We will hear YWCA again too.)

She would do her best to keep me close as much as she could, even changing my outfits several times per day. I have memories of riding in her blue Datsun B-210 to and from work and her smoking her Kool cigarettes and wearing her large afro and red suede jumpsuit. I watched my mother serve the public all the way through my childhood, from teacher, to counselor, to preacher, and to many titles between, but she was always my mom, my friend, and my heart.

Now let's talk about the man who made me the man I am today. That's my best man at my wedding, one of my true role models of being a man, and that's my father known to many as a guy with no cut cards. Now my father had a completely different upbringing than my mother. His father and mother did not have or show what my mother had experienced growing up. Talk about opposites attracting? My father, let's say, came from a broken home where he had memories of being called to come get his mother from a bar for fighting to feeling that his own father betrayed him at an early age. He had three sisters and one brother whom I, till this day, remain very close to and adore. My father, with minimum formal education, had a PhD in the streets and was respected like a real-life Tony Soprano. This man had the work ethic of a military general and the business savvy of a Bill Gates without a completed formal education. I recall him working as a laborer in a plastic plant for a number of years. After his business desires for self-employment became greater, he opened a pool hall in downtown Annapolis, Maryland, which would later become today's primetime real estate in the city. This is important because during this time, there were but five to six black businessmen in Annapolis. They had liquor stores, small corner stores, pool rooms, clubs, bail-bonding businesses, and real estate. Oh, let's not forget fish, produce, insurance, and the numbers game, which is now called the state lottery!

My parents would, through my childhood, own and operate various businesses to include a tropical fish store, restaurant, transportation companies (both limousine and cab), oriental rugs, and even jewelry business. I will break each down as we move through my life.

There were several other key figures in my life as a young man that I must mention early. My father had a lot of people that knew him, but few were what I would call his close friends that would be significant in my life.

The first is a man that to this day, I still call Uncle. He was a career Navy-enlisted guy that I treated like a second dad. As he traveled the world, he would keep me in mind and always bring things back for me, and even when I would announce later in life I would join the Army and while slightly disappointed in my branch choice, he would work with me to ensure that I could properly salute and march, that's my main man, Uncle Harold. Then there is Uncle Harry who I also admired as he worked for a government agency for years and traveled the world. He was a very large, distinguished, grey-bearded, bald man who I watched until his untimely death. My love for him allowed me to later in life take his son Lil Harry under my wing as my nephew and treat him like his dad treated me.

Then, there is Mr. Wright who was another business genius. His son Robbie and I were tight as our dads spent a lot of time together. I recall one night while home alone, as our parents were out, we decided to throw rocks and shoot BB guns from the backyard, and somehow, we hit a car full of four white bicker guys. We ran like hell back into the house to safety. About five to ten minutes went by and they were trying to kick the back door in to come get us. At some point, we made a decision—yes, here we go with making decisions—to run out of the back door through the woods to make it to the 7-Eleven stores. Once inside, I yelled to the clerk to call 911 for help. Police arrived immediately and somehow so did my father; to this day, I don't recall calling him, but he responded like the police. As the police were placing one man into the car in cuffs, my father was trying to remove him from the vehicle to let him know they picked the wrong kid to come after. Another significant man was my cousin's father, Big Jim, who was a career jail warden and had a very strict hand or stick, I should say. My cousins and I would go back and forth spending the night at each other's houses like we lived together. Because of this, when it came time to issue punishment for the smallest of things, I would be caught in the midst. While my parents did not do spanking or beating, Big Jim would lay wood, belt, or branch at the snap of a finger. My cousins (Carlos, Jamie, and later Lil Juan came along). My cousin Carlos was like a real-life Dennis the Menace. If there were specific things we were asked not to do, that would be the only thing Carlos would want us to do. In most cases, he would do it, and we would all get blamed, and of course, poor Jamie would take the beating like a champ as I would be forced to watch. Sometimes, I called my mother and just say, "Come get me, they got whooped again."

Now understand something, we were middle-class people, and my father had both white and black friends with diverse backgrounds. There was another good friend whom I will call Uncle Bruce, a modest white guy full of energy and a magnetic personality. Bruce had a beautiful wife and, later, two kids. This guy was straight about business and would later serve time for his illegal business dealings.

Then there were the Green Brothers, George and Ed. Now, George was a guy who was deep into boxing in the streets from NYC to Baltimore and everywhere in between. He worked with some of the best fighters of all times. He would spend time working on my development of using my hands to defend myself and was convinced that someday, I could be the champ. His brother Ed was the calm, level-headed guy who could meet you once and, five years later, tell you your birthday and maybe even the tag number of your car. These are just a few men who would have influence over my young life. As I grew older, my father had men that would surround him to serve very specific roles. Some of these guys would become like big brothers and uncles to me as I was only the only child for nearly ten years. Big Brother Sammy was one of these early on. I will explain more about each later. Sammy was good with his hands both for fighting and also had OCD for cleanliness. He kept his cars, house, and clothes clean and pressed at all times. He was a staple in the community for a summer basketball league. Then there was a quiet gentleman I called Big Brother Cup. This guy would do any and everything for my father and the team to keep things clean and organized. My father also had a main man or lieutenant we called TJ, and this guy would take a bullet for my father literally; he called my father Pops.

Okay, now, I laid a foundation for a few people in my early teen life; some of these guys had been in prison or would go to prison at some point in my life. Let's start to dissect who I would become and how. You have an opportunity to see an array of backgrounds and people, and as we move forward, it should be easier to understand how well rounded I will become and how well I would learn right from wrong and how to make solid decisions.

TRANSITION TO MANHOOD

O NE YEAR DURING SPRING OR early summer, maybe 1982, just prior to school ending, I was out at a party where I had been working as a DJ duo called the Body Rock Crew. My main man and best friend Thurman was DJ Go. When I arrived home, my father was a bit disheveled, and I didn't know why. When I asked what he was doing up at 2:30 in the morning, he replied, "I just received a weird phone call, and I'm just making sure all the windows are locked."

This didn't make any sense to me at all, and I took a shower and lay down. Just as I would doze off, my sleep was broken by a lot of yelling and cursing, and as I went to sit up, my door flew open with a man racking a 12-gauge sawed-off shotgun in my face, telling me not to be a hero and do what he said. At gunpoint, he brought me out of the room where I now see my father covered in blood where he had been struck over the head with the handle of a gun and my youngest brother Kizza being held by another man holding a large pistol, maybe a 44 magnum, to him, demanding my father to give them money. My mother was standing there partially dressed, begging for the man to give her child to her. My father told me to come into his room where he kept a stash of money from last night's closing of his club. I went and gave the three men some money inside the safe. They pulled all phones out of walls and, at gunpoint, escorted my father down to the cellar. After about one minute, I used a phone in the room they missed because of it being concealed like a wooden box to call the police. I waited a few moments as I could hear the men running into the woods, and I grabbed a shotgun and began checking on my family. I could hear my father's voice very faintly and went to let him out of the cellar where they escorted him down and ordered him to stay until they were out of the house or they would kill us all. I went outside and fired the shotgun into the woods several times until it was empty, praying, yes, praying they were hiding where I was shooting and would hit one of them. My father had been struck with a pistol, and as you know, head wounds bleed very badly. The family regrouped as the police and paramedics arrived, and my father was transported to the hospital.

I went to school the next day, and as you can imagine between the local papers and news and the neighborhood guys talking about what I should have done, I was angry and on edge, walking around like a time bomb waiting to explode. School ended a few weeks later, and my parents thought it would be a good idea for me to go to Jamaica with Uncle Bruce (whom I spoke of earlier) and his family and a freelance photographer who was working for a popular magazine to shoot the Reggae Sun Splash. So I agreed to go and clear my head.

NOT AGAIN

*I*T'S NOW EARLY SUMMER 1982 and I'm headed to Jamaica to relax and get some time to get my head together and calm down from the trauma of a violent home invasion and the mental stress and thoughts of revenge and anger I felt.

We landed in Jamaica, and we got our bags and some big cases full of toys and clothes for the local kids, which was something that Uncle Bruce would take down on each trip. We were stopped at the gate by the Jamaican police, and they proceed to open up boxes of toys and containers which were filled with water guns that would be dumped out onto the floor, and they would begin to break them up and say the water guns can't be allowed in. Now one of the officers would call me Baldy as we were shuffled around and dealt with the confusion of the toys and our bags. This is significant because we will hear this name called again shortly.

Once we arrive at the house which sat up on top of a mountain nearly overlooking all of Montego Bay, we got settled in and began to do what we came to do and that was to relax. After I unpacked my things, I walked down the steps to a lower level where a large swimming pool that overlooked the city of Montego Bay just below the highest patio. As I lay by the pool, Uncle Bruce and the others would say, "We feel safe with you down there" as if I was a security person at the pool on watch. After a few hours of relaxing and a great meal, I retired to bed with my cassette player and headphones.

Just as I dozed off, I'm awakened by loud arguing and commotion, and a loud pop of what sounded like a gunshot! I say to myself, "There is no way in hell, this shit is not happening again!"

At this point, I decide to go into a Jack and Jill bathroom for my own safety and not play hero. After assessing the bathroom as not safe, I realized my closet would be a better and safer place. I go into the closet which has the louver type doors where I can see out but you can't see inside unless you open the doors and look in. Once inside, I hear a man with a strong accent say, "Find Baldy, mon. Find Baldy, mon."

I know they are looking for me because I had heard this name given to me at the airport by the police, and now, I see a shadow enter my room, walking slowly with gun in hand, so I stop my breathing and tuck deep to the right side of the closet and then remained very still, I mean, still as a corpse, like dead person still. I watched the man as he looks in my dresser for valuables and under the mattress and then under the bed, most likely for me now. Now I can see his shadow as he slowly walks toward the closet and opens slowly and puts his head into the closet and looks only to the left, and at the same time, he gets called by his fellow intruders.

"Come now, come now, let's go," the voice says and he runs out of the room. I take a deep breath and sit still for about two minutes, maybe fifteen to thirty, who was counting, right? At some point, I can hear Uncle Bruce and others calling me to come out. Only after I decide it's safe for me, I exit the closet and come out to the living area, only to find everyone tied up face down on the floor, but unharmed! We all regroup and police are notified. Once police are at the house, my gut and everyone else's gut is that this was set up at the airport for sure.

MY DECISION TO LEAVE

I DECIDE IMMEDIATELY THAT AT SUN-UP, I wish to be taken to the airport to return home to my own family in case this is something that may happen again. Hell, if I'm going to go through this, I should at least be home with my own family, right? The police request that I stay and clear their investigation and then leave afterward.

"Crap, I didn't need a masters in criminal justice to see this was an inside job", so I'm saying to myself and out loud, "Investigate what?"

I again explain that at sunrise, I am headed to the airport. I'm out. So within just under thirty to forty-eight hours, I return home to my family. Since my friends and Cousin Jamie expected me to be gone for two weeks, when I walked into the summer league game ready to play ball, they thought I was a Derek double. I shared my story and all were floored.

MY FATHER PREPARES ME
FOR REAL MANHOOD

ONE DAY SHORTLY AFTER MY return, as all my friends are all outside playing basketball in our yard, my father pulled into the driveway in his black Benz and parked and went into the house. After a few minutes, he called out in a special way of his window to me, "Derek, come in here for a min."

As I entered his room, he sat on the edge of his bed and said, "Close the door and sit down."

I did as he said and I could tell he was bothered by something serious. My father looked at me and said, "I'm proud of you and believe you are a strong young man and some things are about to happen that will force you to step up and handle some things around here."

It was as if he was about to tell me he was dying or something. It was just a long pause and something said to me, "Don't ask," so I didn't.

He said, "You know how to run Portside." That was his restaurant and prized possession. "You also know where I keep all the money, who to trust, so be ready to step up."

I said, "Okay," and he let me walk out. After about ten minutes, he left, still with the blank face, and all my boys asked if everything was okay. And I said, "Yeah, I guess."

Approximately an hour or two later, the phone rang in the house and I ran to answer it, and it was my Uncle Jessie, my father's brother. And with a frantic voice, he said, "Your father has just shot two people in town."

I was confused and didn't have a clue of what to say. My uncle said he was coming to the house to explain.

I would shortly find out that my father shot the two men, one of whom he had reason to believe played a role in us being victims of the home invasion, and the other man, as it would later come out, was a victim of being in the wrong place at the wrong time. I would also later find out that my father did this and drove himself to the police station and told them he had just done it.

The bottom line is you did not mess with his family and that he would go to any length to send that message to anyone who did.

As the legal process would begin and news spread and I continued to play music for parties and move about town, interestingly enough, I would now be viewed as Rob's son and also feared and respected as well.

My mother and I now would begin our work as a team in getting the daily business of opening and closing the restaurant and tag teaming my school and the load of handling my siblings and their care. I would go to school and do football, track, and basketball practice, then after getting home handling kids and then head across the Bay Bridge to work for a few hours and my mother would come later and I would either stay with her or go home to my siblings. This process would show later to become my role as a big brother on a whole other level.

My father bought in a young powerhouse lawyer we will call Billy, and his master of courtroom drama would get my father a short sentence to include work release toward the end because of his business ownership. Now interestingly enough, through all of this, I had decided to do a delayed entry into the Army reserves, and I must tell you, my father initially was not happy. So much so that he denied the recruiter access to our home. My mother's authority and power of attorney overruled and I was given a report date to attend basic training in Fort Dix, New Jersey, prior to graduation in June of 1984. Once I had officially enlisted, my father had also officially been pushed over the edge by my actions. He sat me down to ask why I had done this. When I responded with my answer, it was not a proper one. My answer was that I wanted to travel. He came back with I could see the world without joining the military, but if this was my decision, while he did not like it or support it, I should now know that once I leave, I was not to ask for anything regarding his support ever again.

Several days later, my father would call me in with a complete change of heart and, during another sit-down, not only to apologize for what he previously said, but also that he would tell me that he supported me 100 percent and wished me all the best, saying he knew I would do well.

In early December of 1983, I would depart for Fort Dix, New Jersey, for basic training for the Army Reserves. The morning I left, a good friend of mine came to the house on a quick leave between his basic and advanced individual training to warn me we had been lied to by our recruiter. I believe he was upset because of his ASFAB scores, not allowing him to get the job he really wanted, but he made out okay.

I arrived at Fort Dix and would have a blast in basic training. The next couple of months would be what I needed to get away. Shortly after I departed, my father would also begin his prison sentence, which would force my mother to be alone, with four kids and a business. I recall at basic training graduation, my mother and only grandparent (my father's mother), Grandma Memo or Grandma Mary, would attend with my Uncle Jessie.

After graduation, I would go to Fort Rucker, Alabama, for school to learn how to work on UH-1 helicopters. My school would expose me to a whole different culture. After attending private schools and predominately white public schools, I was used to interacting with white people on a normal and friendly/regular basis. Once in Alabama, I was exposed to some of the most blatant racism I could have ever imagined. A few of my barrack friends had come from areas of the country where they were not only used to it, they were also used to fighting to express their displeasure with it. I dealt with it with a few minor altercations, but it was something I felt I could handle.

While on a short leave while rehabbing a left knee scope, I ran into a family member who coached football at Bowie State and explained the ROTC program to me. After hearing about it and hearing about the potential to even play football, I was interested in following through with the offer of a split ROTC and football scholarship. Upon completion of school and arrival to my reserve unit, I was registered and ready to become a student at Bowie State. Now interestingly enough as an enlisted and somewhat one-year veteran, you couldn't tell me anything. So during my arrival on the campus of Bowie State, I headed to meet the commander. I encountered a young soldier who stopped to question why I did not salute him! I was taken back and somewhat irritated by his tone, and after a quick view, an interesting conversation took place. He assumed I was a new cadet and he did not see my enlisted private rank, but I did see his three silver dots and had no clue what they meant. So after a pleasant exchange, he guided me to the captain's office. After getting an overview of the program, I would go meet the football coach and hear about the rebuilding that was on the horizon. I was sold on Bowie and could not wait to start in the fall semester of the next year.

I had purchased a blue Toyota sports car with a sunroof and loaded to the hill for that time. Also right after getting it, I received a speeding ticket and ignored the court date. My mother decided one afternoon to ride all the way to Ocean City to see a tarot card reader and satisfy some curiosity. As we made the drive, just Mom and me, like old times, we laughed and joked, and upon arriving, I sat in the car or stayed close while she was inside.

It's what comes next that's the mind blower.

My mother gets in the car and remains very quiet and begins to partially laugh while also appearing confused. She starts to talk, but only after a long disclaimer that was told not to share with anyone after leaving. She starts off with asking me about my speeding ticket as if she knew something. The lady told her something about each person in the house and she said specifically that her oldest son had just purchased a sports car that would later cause him problems because after an accident, a ticket would be an issue. She said that her son (me) was going to someday marry a teacher and oversee lots of people and also be followed by many people.

The lady also suggested that someone close to my mother was away from her in a dark place and that she was very sad, and she told the lady it was my father who was in prison. At some point, the lady said that someone close, very close, to our family unit was responsible for the cloud that was hovering over our family household and that this person also was responsible for the men coming into our home. My mother said the lady asked if she wanted her to say who specifically it was, but she didn't allow her. (To this day, I don't know if she chose to just not tell me, but years later, I would find out.) What's very significant is that she told my mother that she would one day speak to and lead hundreds of gathered people. She told my mother that she too possessed some supernatural abilities but was afraid to speak of them. She told my mother that's why she came a long way to verify some things she had been envisioning but couldn't get clarity on. After my mother explained various other things about their sitting, we enjoyed our ride back and promised that we would share our dreams and visions with each other for life. About two weeks later, I would share with my mother that a friend of mine was killed in an accident, and for a couple of weeks, I would have a recurring dream that someone was trapped in a car and couldn't get out after having an accident. She would ask what I thought it was, and I had no idea because I could never see their face.

YET ANOTHER GAME CHANGER

*M*Y MOTHER BECAME A PARTNER with a girlfriend of hers and opened a childcare center where I would work as an aide for all the teachers and handled activities with the kids through the spring and coming summer. On this particular day, she would ask me to do a bank run for her and come right back to assist with dismissal. She handed me the bank bag with checks to deposit, and I walked out to my car, and as I opened the door, one of the teacher's aides that I had been joking with jumped in my car as if she would be going with me as well. I requested that she not go and that I would be right back. I departed the child care center and drove no more than a mile, and as I was just about to initiate a left turn after waiting for oncoming traffic to stop, at some point, a man waved me on to make my turn. Neither he nor I realized that another car in the far lane was still traveling at a high rate of speed and would be broadsided/T-boned on the passenger side of my car. I remember clutching the wheel and bracing for impact, and I can recall the first of at least two rollovers before my vehicle would come to rest approximately fifty feet from impact.

Now this trip should have taken no more than fifteen minutes there and back, so after about thirty to forty minutes, and several parents being late picking up their kids, it was one parent who says to my mother that there was a bad accident up the street, some jackass has flipped a sports car over, and they are cutting them out of the car and it doesn't look good. My mother's heart dropped, and she demanded someone take her to the scene.

As she approaches, she notices that the emergency personnel have a sheet held up as if they are about to cover a body, and she sees it's my car and me they are working on. She melts as she begins to process that her firstborn child may be dead. Later that day, I would be awake and conscious enough to hear her voice and feel her hand on my head and say, "Suga, can you hear me?"

At the same time, we would smile and say, "The dream and the lady," proving we were on the same thought process at the moment. Shortly after me getting enough strength to talk and walk, a few emergency responders who worked on me wished me all the best and explained how they couldn't believe I survived such a wreck. They said had anyone been in the passenger seat, they would have died for sure. They said the passenger door was pressing into me on the driver's side panel. The responding police also arrived to issue me a few citations, one of which was failure to yield right of way and the other was failing to appear for a speeding ticket. They laughed and said it was clear I was not going anywhere and to pay the fines or come to court. My mother and I both looked at each other and smiled with a sense of peace that God had looked over me.

HERE IS SOME NEWS FOR YOU

*A*S IF BEING LAID UP from an accident was not enough, here comes some more interesting news from one of the favorite cousins of my heart, Quay. After some small talk, she reveals to me that a young lady whom I had spent some time with had just had a baby and was living in California, and I responded by saying, "That's cool, good for her, I guess."

After a short pause, Quay repeats to me that the young lady had a new baby and she then laughs again. As my heart dropped and fingers started counting, I began to process the inside joke. Could this be true? I immediately called her and asked her for the update, and she did tell me she had a baby and that she even named her after my sister Eshe, but she still never initially came out and said I was the father. She would remain in California for nearly two years before I would see this little girl. I will come back to this later.

I am now about to head to my first semester at Bowie State. The interesting thing now is being creative enough to make up the balance for books and housing that the scholarships didn't cover. My mother (God love her) would offer up a choice credit card for books, but I would need to quickly come up with money for the next semester. So I dove right into making money mode by promoting live shows from groups we used at our restaurant a few years back and also keep my father's limo business as a way of income. I would provide limo service to homecoming acts like Mickey Howard, Phyllis Hyman, Anita Baker, and others.

My roommate Dave was an interesting character but had a heart of gold. My first semester, I was in my room for two weeks, no roommate, and one day as I went to my room, three of my closest boys were in the hall laughing at my arrival. I had no idea why, but it was clear the joke was on me. As I entered the room, this student who looked too old to be in school with about a ten-inch afro says to me, "Yo, yo, you must be D-ski!"

I replied, "No, I'm Derek and pleased to meet you."

His reply was "Word."

By now, Deco, AJ, and Joey were in stitches, laughing at this conversation that would last about ten minutes. I understood not a single word he said, it was as if he spoke another language. Dave would move in and get settled, and we would become great friends. I would have ROTC physical training in the early mornings, and Dave kept stats for all athletics on campus and would come in late. 307 Holmes Hall would become the room to hang out at on our floor.

Later in the semester, I would get a job at the Pentagon through a stay-in-school work program and get a taste of a government job and star power of being in the Pentagon. I worked deep in the basement reproducing secret and classified documents for the Joint Chiefs. During this time, some of us even went to UPS part-time as well to earn extra money, and it lasted about two months before the hard labor forced us all to quit one night after two-a-day football practices.

As time would progress, I decided, just before going to advance camp for juniors at Fort Bragg, I would get an off-campus apartment in Laurel. I signed a lease and the weekend before I left on that Monday was all I had before I departed for six to eight weeks. So a young lady or the primary young lady I was seeing volunteered to move my stuff in and keep watch over my place while I was gone. What a mistake! After returning from camp, I entered my apartment, only to find that it appeared it was a woman's place. There were pink dishes and all types of girlie stuff everywhere. This young lady had made this her home. The relationship did not last very long as it was full of drama, and many more would come and go until sometime in late 1988, there would be a shift. I was introduced by a coworker to two young ladies at the same time, one of whom he had begun dating just two weeks prior to introducing me to them both. As we approached the car, they arrived outside our job (which was another government contract security). We approached the passenger side. Now picture this—he does not tell me who is who. He goes to the driver side and left me at the passenger side. As my eyes fixed on the cute West Indian passenger, we began talking, and after an exchange of names, he and the driver laugh and tell me I was to come to meet the driver! Very disappointed at first, I proceed around the car to meet this older cutie from New York. We hit it off very quickly and finding out they were roommates along with one other younger lady (all were Howard students).

So my coworker and I began to go over together to visit the girls, but the attraction from the first eye contact did not go away. After about three months, there was an argument between me and the young lady I was seeing, so she confided in her roommate to call and speak some sense into me. When the roommate called me at work, her call was transferred to my post and she and I began talking, it was about me and her roommate for about ten minutes and we cut to the chase. She and my coworker had broken it off, so I went to him to let him know to get his approval, and with his arrogance and hurt feelings from their quick breakup, he said he was okay with me speaking to her and pursuing her further.

So our demonic scheme would begin. Initially, I would send one of my best friends, my main man in the world, Vince, to pick her up in his tricked-out Suzuki truck while I sat in the back and then he would take us to my car at the job and we would go to my apartment. Well, this went on for months. One long weekend (holiday), her two roommates went to New York and were not due back till Monday. So Friday and Saturday night, I stayed over. Well, Sunday, while in the shower, I could hear a loud conversation, so I assumed she was on the phone, and as I exited the bathroom with only a towel around me, there were both roommates in the hall! At this point, I was breaking up a possible disaster in the making. After being cursed and nearly attacked, we packed and departed the house and went to my apartment. While she seemed to not really be bothered, I had a bit of emotion of guilt for my part in hurting someone's feelings who really liked me. So after morning came and I looked out my kitchen window, I noticed a letter on my car. I went out to retrieve it. The letter told us both we deserved each other and wished us well. The relationship lasted about one solid year and hit rock bottom and I asked her to leave. She partially left and stayed with a couple for a few months and jumped right back in the game hard and fast, which was more than I could handle of both drama and women. Now at some point again, I began to have too much drama as the one who departed 1.5 years back kept showing up on my step late at night like a lost cat.

I began to spend a lot of time with one in particular, and after a few months and knowing about my sisters getting their done in Annapolis, she asked about where they got their hair done and they suggested the shop in Annapolis where they went.

LOVE UNDER NEW MANAGEMENT

*M*AKING THIS HAIR APPOINTMENT WOULD change my life forever! The appointment was made and the date that would change my life is now in an appointment book. I would drop her off with the intention of picking her up and taking her back to my house so I could attend a Martin Luther King dinner with my mother that evening.

Okay, when I arrived at the salon and parked, I could see her at the counter and she seemed to be talking as if something was wrong and this went on for a good while, so I went in to check. I found that as I walked in the shop, there was a woman stylist in the first chair on the right side of the door that had on a cute outfit and some purple suede shoes and she was fine as a $10,000 bottle of wine. As I got a grip and my eyes back on the pending issue, which turned out to be that she was not happy with her hair and didn't want it done over, but expected me to pay for it. I agreed to pay only if she had whoever did it redo it so she could be happy. After we cleared the issue of her not being satisfied with her hair that another stylist had done, we left, and on the ride home, she asked me if I noticed the stylist on the right and how well dressed and attractive she was. Very smoothly, I replied, "Yes, I think I saw her too," and that's all I said. Once back at my house and in a very tactful haste, I advised my female friend that I needed to shower and change my clothes for my event and would speak to her later. This was my polite way of saying, "Please hurry and leave."

Once she left, I called my sister Eshe to quickly inquire as to whom the very attractive lady in the shop was. My sister got very excited and said her name was Carla. My sister seemed to be excited that I asked. I changed and I arrived at my parents' home and went straight upstairs to my father and told him, "I met my wife today."

He laughed, and I explained to him this woman was definitely the one for me, I could just feel it. My mother was now ready, and on the ride over to the event, we discussed my excitement over my seeing my future "bride." She laughed and we discussed my plan, which I did not yet have.

The next day, at roll call in the Special Response Team (SRT) squad room, I announced to the entire team I had met my wife, and of course, there was major laughter because my reputation with women had me pegged as the least likely to ever be married. After two long days, I decided to make an appointment to have my hair cut and washed by another stylist so I could see this future wife of mine again. Once I entered the salon on my appointment day, I glanced over at her, and again, this weird feeling overwhelmed me as if I could not speak. The lady cut and washed my hair, and while in the shampoo bowl, I could see her walk by and my heart was just racing. After the lady was done with my hair, I left the salon, trying to figure out my game plan. Now day 4, I decided today was the day to man up and just call her. I dialed the number, and when the phone was answered, I asked to speak with her. She answered the call with a hello I will never forget. Now I had her on the phone, I said, "This is Derek, Eshe and Carrie's older brother."

She replied, "I know exactly who it is," and she chuckled as if she was blushing!

I said, "It's taken me four days to do this, so if you would accept a lunch invitation, I would love to take you to lunch."

She replied, "Sure!"

I nearly jumped to the ceiling with joy. We set a date for the next Monday as most salons are closed on Mondays. We decided to meet at a place called Bennagins in Laurel, Maryland. We sat and began conversation, and the waitress, a little cutie herself, decides she would pick today to flirt with me, and on my first outing with what I already claimed as my future bride, I get a fresh waitress. Carla, being a great sport, caught it and laughed it right off.

I was due at work for a 3–11 p.m. shift and it's now 2:45 p.m., and we are still sitting at the table, so I call my lieutenant (Lt. Larry). Lt. Larry answers the phone and I tell him I'm going to be late.

He replied, "Let me guess, you're with your future wife?"

I said, "Yes, sir."

He told me to take the day off and good luck!

After the extended lunch was over, we departed and decided to go to Baltimore in a couple of days for lunch.

Second meeting: We went to Baltimore City Inner Harbor for a good lunch and then decided to take a ride on the paddle boats. So we had a week to chat on the phone a few times and now our second date. While on the paddle boat, my soon-to-be bride decides to see if I have a real sense of humor and tells me she has two daughters. I didn't know what to say, so to myself, I said, "I knew this was too good to be true!"

After I paused, I asked how old they were and where are they?

She laughed and said, "I'm joking, I have two nieces that are like my own."

I laughed and thanked God. During this time, I had a little girl that was 3.5 years old that was my little heart. Her name was Ashay. There were a few encounters with her mom, and when she became pregnant, she packed up and moved to California without notice, but she is here now and she is my heart.

I laughed and then explained to her that I found out about her when one of my cousins told me that the woman had a child, and that child was mine. I first saw her when she was two years old and immediately began treating her as my own. My future bride would also immediately take pride and love her as she was a part of me too.

After our date at the Inner Harbor, we returned to my apartment and sat and talked for a few hours. When she went to leave, we stood at the door talking for another fifteen to twenty minutes, and my issue was I wanted to kiss her, but was afraid I would come off too fast, so I just said good-bye, closed the door, and placed my back to the door, puzzled at what and when to cross the line. This door game would continue for over a month, maybe two, of speaking and seeing each other on a regular basis.

We decided to hit a jazz show at Blues Alley and go meet a friend of mine and a few others while his uncle performed. After dinner and the show, we returned to my place again, and this night at the door, I decided I would just move in and get it over with. Bam! First kiss has landed! Okay, we are good! She laughed and jokingly said, "What took you so long?"

I knew after all those long good-byes where I was going next. After a few more outings, I would be at her house, and one of her good friends Pam would show up at her house allegedly unannounced, but clearly to check me out! I fell in love with Pam like a sister immediately.

TIME TO MEET MOMMY GRAY

*W*E DECIDED TO GO MEET her mom for the first time, and while excited, I was a bit nervous as this was a big step for a guy who had been out there like I was. As we get to the door, her mom opens the door, and as Carla walks in, she says to her mom, "We can't stay long because he has to get home to his wife!"

Her mom said, "His what?"

I immediately said, "Mom, she is joking, I am not married."

After my nerves recovered from the bad joke and had met both Mom and Dad, they felt like family and this was great. Mr. Gray, Pop Pop, was a man of very few words, but would have a heart bigger than anyone I knew.

The courtship would continue and grow as we both would still need to do some house cleaning of our previous relationships. I had the issue with the live-in who still needed to move on, and she still had an ex lurking in my shadows who I would have to have a heart to heart with. As months went on, I finally asked one evening if she would spend the night, and after she pondered for a short moment, she asked me to retrieve an overnight bag from her car (Louie Vuitton, of course). Now my decision to be a real gentleman is really tough, so I just let the universe take control. I decided the first night to just hold and cuddle and think sports, cars, and anything to control my hormones! LOL. The next morning was Monday and she was off, so we just hung out relaxing until my 3 p.m. shift would start.

As more time would go on, we would go back and forth between her place and mine. Now you recall I said a while back, I still had a part-time live-in who said we needed to move on with our lives, and now the time has come to begin to get my life in order and close some loose ends. It's now time for me to take some action to show this woman whom I have already decided is going to someday be my wife.

Of course, during this time, this is where I would be tested in many ways. The young lady whom I took to the salon was very respectful early and moved on with her life after she stopped by one day unannounced after a date with Carla, and saw congratulations balloons for my promotion to lieutenant on the tactical team. She read the card and asked was this woman from the salon and I said yes. She asked were we getting serious, and with a straight face, I said, "Yes, I think I'm going to marry her." She was hurt, but left very respectful.

Now the part-time live-in was a different story. When she received the news, she prepared to dig in and arm herself for battle! And the next few months would change me in many ways. I recall prior to one birthday weekend, Carla would request I be free from Thursday to Sunday, and she was clear not to ask why! Now let me paint this picture clear for you. I'm in love with a woman I'm 100 percent sure I want to be my wife, and yes, I still have a woman technically living in my home as a part-time roommate/former girlfriend. I have decided somewhere in this twisted maze of emotions I need a fast motorcycle, so I go out and hunt for a motorcycle. I found one and decide I'm going to put some money on it to hold for two weeks while I get my funds together and share this only with Carla. Okay, so the week prior to Carla's request to be free for Thursday to Sunday, the part-time ex-girlfriend is at the house all week. When I get in Wednesday from working a 7–3 p.m. shift, there are like two other couples in my apartment enjoying a happy hour and preparing for dinner, and I'm the host for the night! I go into the room and ask one of the brothers, a good friend of mine, to step in the room to talk to him. Once the door closes, I ask him to tell me what's going on! He advises me they were all invited and that my part-time live-in has been cooking all day and has taken this evening very serious! I advised him I have plans and need to be somewhere! At that moment she says, "Dinner is ready," and now at the same time, Carla begins to call, and I'm so confused, I can't think straight!

BAD DECISION MADE

I DECIDED TO DEAL WITH WHAT'S in front of me and sit down for dinner instead of taking Carla's call. After dinner, there is still company and ongoing conversation, and Carla has called several times and I have not answered a single call during the evening. Morning comes, and finally, I begin to call Carla back and all day no answer. So at some point, I decide to go to the dealer and put the money down on the bike to have something to relieve some tension. Upon my arrival, I immediately noticed a "Sold" tag on the motorcycle, and now I'm pissed! Two salesmen come over laughing and said, "Try tomorrow because some lady had come in and paid cash for it for her boyfriend and all he had to do today was show up to get fitted for a helmet, but she had called early that morning and said she would be coming to get her money back, and she seemed pissed at the boyfriend. What a dumbass he must have been to have a woman do that and he does something to blow it!"

OUT WITH THE EXPLANATION

*L*ATER THAT EVENING, I WOULD speak to Carla and attempt to explain what happened Wednesday night. She advised me to let her know when I got myself together; she would be waiting. It was also here where she would tell me we had a trip to the Bahamas and we would have left Thursday afternoon, but only after picking up my new motorcycle! Yes, I was the dumbass the salesman spoke of. They didn't know it was me, and I never suspected Carla was the girlfriend they spoke of.

So I must sit the live-in down and talk and resolve this living situation, so I can move on. When she came in and I attempted to speak, there was major drama before I could get it all out. Since she caught the metro bus to my house, I would be forced to take her to the couple's house she had been staying with on occasion. On the way over, there was another West Indian explosion in the car, and once I pulled into the couple's house, she refused to exit the car, so I got out, getting the couple to come get her, and as I exited the car, she locked the doors and proceeded to kick my windshield out! After the windshield was completely destroyed, she exited the vehicle and ran. We were able to eventually calm her down and get her into their house. Since I was close to my job, I called to advise the job I would be leaving my car at the job overnight for a morning windshield repair. I also advised her she has about forty-eight hours to remove all her personal belongings from my home or they would be placed by the Dumpster.

The next day after work as I entered my home, she was packing, and when I asked if she needed a hand, she stated she could no longer stay with the couple (most likely because of what they saw), but she would be staying with my parents. Yes, my parents and she advised me that Mother was on her way to get her! When I looked up, my mother was in my doorway to pick her up! Now, my mother would have the biggest heart in the world and would take an ax murderer in if God told her to, but I'm saying to myself, "Mom, please don't do this!" My mother said she was shocked at my behavior and could not believe I could be so mean.

I would now ask both Mom and the young lady to please leave so I could assess the damage done and regroup. Later that night, I would notice clothing of mine that had been cut up! At this point, I ensured all her remaining items were by the door to be removed forthwith from my home. A few days later, she returned, and I would extend the olive branch to take her and her belongings to my mother's since I was going that way. On the ride down, she went into another rage and began to throw my CDs out the window and also destroy my stereo head unit. I pulled in to park and exited the vehicle to get her to calm down. After a few minutes, I decided to stoop to her level and take her TV out and throw it on the parking lot to get her attention and let her know I had enough. When I got back in to the car, there was calm for about two minutes and then another eruption. My next stop was to the District II Prince Georges County Police Station, where I went inside and asked for some assistance and to also have a record of this unfolding drama. They advised it was not much they could do, but agreed to at least walk out and speak to her as a professional courtesy. After she calmed down, I proceeded to my mother's and dropped her off.

After a few days of calm in the personal waters of my own soap opera, I would go on a dinner date with Carla to a nice seafood restaurant in DC by the wharf, and we have a great evening and begin to work back into rhythm. As we exited the parking lot, my car phone begins to ring and it's someone I had no contact with since meeting Carla, and when I see the number, I decide not to answer. (Now this is in the days when your phone was mounted in your car.) At some point, I did answer, and the young lady said she wanted to see me and I said I was out and thanks for calling and hung up. She proceeded to ask if I had someone in the car with me and that she really wanted to talk and come see me and if some bitch was with me, she needed to just deal with it while we talked. I hung up. The phone continued to ring and ring and ring. I finally unplugged the headset, but the base kept ringing. By now, Carla is saying, "Let me answer it and handle it."

Now Carla was the calm, mellow, non-combative type, but this woman calling was certifiable crazy when mad, and I did not want to go there. Eventually, she stopped calling. What had been her issue was when Carla said to call her when I got myself together. I went through my lil black book and called folks to say I was moving on and some I left voice mails for on answering machines and did not take the return calls and disposed of the lil black book. This one was calling to make a booty call and wanted me to know how pissed she was when she was left a message and then I refused to return her calls.

CARLA'S PAST DID NOT GO WITHOUT A FIGHT!

I RECALL DURING OUR COURTSHIP WAKING up one morning to her phone ringing, and when I answered with hello, I got a "Who is this?"

Of course, I responded back with "Who is this?"

I quickly explained to the brother that she was not home and that I would be very clear he was to never dial this phone again.

Apparently, he would decide to go to her work for another version of my words from Carla. Once we decided to purchase our first home together, we would find during a credit report that conniving young man had used Carla's name for credit to make purchases of gifts he gave her and also lost an apartment she would be cosigning for.

Sometime later, I would run into this same guy in a nightclub and see him point me out to a group of his buddies. With my short fuse, I would immediately without thought go grab him and escort him out of the club and explain he would pay those debts back immediately or face court proceedings. Shortly afterward, he would be served a subpoena to pay for debts to clear Carla's name.

OKAY, TIME TO GET SERIOUS

*I*T HAD BEEN A YEAR now, and I decide I'm all in now. So I begin the search for, yes, a ring! I am 100 percent plus that this woman is going to be the mother of my kids and be my wife for life! I find a ring, and around October/November, take it straight to her father to ask for his permission to marry his baby girl. He paused and laughed and said, "Sure, I don't see why not!"

I knew then that Christmas would be my big day. So on Christmas Eve, we decided to stay at her place, and around 10–11 p.m., we decided to open a gift a piece before Christmas Day, so I'm ready to do the deed! I get on my knee, my gift in hand, and she opens the box and my heart races 200 miles per hour. When she sees the ring and smiles, I ask her, "Carla, will you be my wife?"

She says yes, and at that moment, I was the happiest guy in the world. She called her older sister Jeanie, Pam, her mom, and maybe a few others too! We decided we would take the year to plan and a date of October, early/midmonth.

LIL ASHAY

*E*ARLY DURING OUR MARRIAGE, WE decided I wanted the best for my little girl and attempted to get custody. After securing an attorney, I learned we first had to prove paternity. I submitted to my blood test immediately, but her mom would not show up for two appointments. During the second hearing, the judge ordered a warrant for the mother's arrest and my heart pleaded with him to not do that, but rather she be allowed one more attempt. Once the results were in, another date was given, and it was on this day my heart would be crushed to find that the little nine-year-old love of my life was not my child. It was like being punched in the nose. I recall calling my mother for advice on what to do. I would now sit down with my little lady and try to explain why I was not her birth father, but would be there as her daddy until the day I die. To this very day, she calls me dad in her own special way (she would now, in 2013, give birth to her own son whom she provides for very well).

WEDDING PLANS

$\mathcal{W}$E DECIDE TO GO BIG and all out as only my queen should have and deserve. We begin our venue search and interviews of photographers, caterers, musicians, and DJs. After we nail all these folks down, we are ready and excited. We decide Aruba would be our honeymoon destination. During this year's planning period, our contracted photographer would do photo shoots of us during all four seasons to put together an incredible show for our guest.

I must make final decisions on my best man, and after processing what a best man stands for or should represent, I decide that friends come and go, and that the only man that would never leave my side was my real-life hero and that my father would be my best man.

The wedding day would come and go on without a mere resemblance of an issue. There were a few funny moments. Just after my queen completely donned her gown and was fully ready to go, she decided she needed to tinkle and did not give herself ample time to make it to the rest room, so needless to say, she had to be freshened up and change her underclothing. Our coordinator, who was like an angel to us and I will refer to her as Mrs. B., she treated us like she was the mom to us who was proud to see people so in love and join together to spend the rest of our lives together. Mrs. B. had an incredible knack for doing things to make you smile or cooking for you to soothe a special taste bud.

During the wedding ceremony, which was an after-6 p.m. affair while the church was packed and the music played, I could not stop thinking of how proud I would be when this day was over, it was as if I was dreaming. My queen stood next to me and had a glow I would never forget.

NEWLYWEDS

*N*OW THAT I OFFICIALLY HAVE the woman of my dreams and future mother of my children, what do I do next?

Well, you can imagine, I began to process she is my wife for life and I must focus on treating her like the queen she deserves to be treated like. We spend an incredible time in Aruba on our honeymoon just enjoying each other's company and our new future together.

We enjoy the next couple of months working on establishing ourselves and discussing bringing children into the world and nurturing them and having an incredible family. Around 1992, we began the real fun of working hard on having children, and while during our period of planning, we were not having the success we had hoped for. In early 1993, after consulting doctors and going through some disappointing months of wondering, we were finally one day looking at a positive pregnancy test! We were so excited. God would really reveal himself to us around the same time as I had been accepted into the Prince Georges County Policy Academy Session #77. So we have a new home and baby on the way, along with a new career start.

GOD'S PLANS ARE NOT ALWAYS OURS

$\mathscr{I}$ RECALL ONE DAY SITTING IN class and being called out by a stern voice, saying, "Matthews, get out here now!"

Once in the hall, my senior instructor placed his hand on my shoulder and advised me to immediately respond to my home to be with my wife! I was scared and emotional as I would find out something was wrong. After our arrival to the hospital, we would be advised that our pregnancy would be a loss and a procedure called a DNC would need to be done! This news crushed both of us, and I immediately began to wonder if all my cruel behavior in playing with people's emotions was now haunting me.

We would take some time over the next year and change to gather ourselves and rebuild our spirits and faith and try again. This would include diet changes to include no red meat, no alcohol, and lots of prayers. Again, sometime in the spring of 1995, my wife, my queen, would come to me with her infectious smile with my dinner on a tray. Tonight would be interesting because this dinner tray would have two bowls on top of it, one blue and one pink. Why this was significant you will soon find out. She did two tests to confirm, and because you don't know sex by these tests, she went with boy and girl colors. We had no idea of the news to come.

I was not prepared for the news to come. Now to really understand the significance of the next piece of information, you need to understand I was about as hardcore as troops go. I mean I could spit fire and eat rusty nails. I had a reputation among the county as a guy that did not play when it came time to go into a real hostile situation.

My queen was very ill at the start of the term, and because of that, it required an overnight stay at the hospital. Early one morning,

I had to leave to execute some warrants with my squad, and afterward, I would get off duty and stop home to shower and wash my car and returned to the hospital to be with by bride.

DOWN FOR THE COUNT

*A*s I washed my car, our phone rang, and as the handset set on the step, my next-door neighbor would answer for me and bring the phone over to me. I dried my hands and took the phone and said hello.

My bride would say, "Hey, Big Daddy," and laugh.

I laughed back and said, "What's up? I'm on my way shortly."

She would reply with "Okay, all four of us will be here when you arrive!"

(Pause.)

I said, "What, who's there with you?"

She replied, "No one's here, just me and three heart beats."

A few moments later, I would find out that I passed out as my neighbors splashed water on me! LOL! I immediately rushed to be with her and we could not have had more joy. As time would progress, she would be extremely ill and require bed rest and special care, and at some point, the third heartbeat would be two strong babies, one boy and one girl. As we prepared for our two bundles of joy, we would prepare to just love them. Over the next nine months, I watched my queen go through many changes mentally, physically, and emotionally, and I would have to dig deep to balance career and home.

WHAT DEFINES A REAL MAN?

EFORE I MOVE ON, LET me break and give you my perspective on how I view love and a real man. Entirely too many folks say love is nearly impossible to understand or better yet, even impossible to define. I say, "Love is action." A real man will love his wife the way the Bible says to love her. No one would ever condemn a man if we loved like the Bible says. Now you recall a while back, I said I was hardcore, right? Note: I never said real man, and here is why.

After doing some serious self-examination while going through my trials, I see that I was not the definition of what a real man was, and I'm not ashamed to say I'm still working on it while writing this book for your use to develop your own strength to achieve your goal as a man.

A real man will treat his wife right. He will be servant rather than a master. He will always do the right thing because it's what he is supposed to do. He will give his wife 100 percent no matter what he is asked to do.

HOW WILL A MAN KNOW WHEN HE IS A REAL MAN?

ẂHEN HE SEEKS TO SERVE. When he can sit down with his queen honestly and look to fulfill her needs before his own. He should ask her "Honey, what can I do for you?" Society says man should find a fine wife who will take care of his needs, make him happy, and serve him. She should become his entire world, make him proud, and he should give her everything he thinks she wants. But she's miserable. She's in second place. He can't put her first because that goes against everything he feels and has been taught. Just like everything else God made perfect, the world has twisted this all up. You see, there is this fake thing being sold to men and the market, and it's called lust!

It's exciting. It looks good. It's even satisfying for a short while. But it's not true love. It's backwards. It fulfills our desires first, even at the expense of the very person we love. There is a huge difference, and we men need to learn and know it. Lust takes for our own gain. Love gives for the benefit of the one we love the most.

MY PRINCE AND PRINCESS ARRIVE

*A*s I STATED EARLIER, WE carefully planned for what I was about to experience. During the early morning of November 30, my queen would awake me to let me know, "Honey, it's time!"

Now I, being calm and the perfect executor of plans and operations, had to be more than ready for this moment. I mean our bags packed, various dry runs because of false alarms, and now it's time. Somehow in the commotion of the moment, I froze! I didn't move fast enough, and between her water breaking and getting her to the car, I forgot our bags and, on the way, missed the hospital exit! Once in the hospital and settled in, I began to reflect on all the excitement, how things went according to God's plan and not mine, which is how life does.

During my law enforcement and life, I have observed parents interact with their children. I have reflected on my observations and processed that there are parents who refer to their kids as an accidental pregnancy or even a surprise. This clear ignorance on the parents' perspective, and I believe it can even affect how they treat a child. Even worse, if a child hears this, it can destroy them. So if you feel this way, keep your mouth shut and that secret to yourself. What you think was a surprise to you as a man or woman was not a surprise in God's eyes. We should thank God he does not have accidents. Then ask yourself what messages are you sending your child? Do your kids you see as a surprise see themselves as burdens or blessings? I don't mean to be so harsh, but if this applies to you and hurts your feelings, you should put this book down right now because I intend to take this even deeper.

Imagine if your successful life you believe is so perfect and God was to come tell you he made a mistake and you had to take on a life of poverty and despair and your self-image would be crushed. How about if your perfect relationship with your spouse and one night over dinner or on vacation, they said, "I wish I had married my high school sweetheart instead of you?" Well, folks, this is what these kids feel and also what God feels when we worship false things!

FAMILY LOVE AND LOVE FOR GOD

*I*T DOES NOT MATTER HOW hard life gets, we all belong with family. Yes, there are going to be times when we let down the people we love the most and who cares the most. The key to family is that when this happens, they are the ones who say, "It's okay, we are only concerned about you, and that's all that matters."

No matter the pain, embarrassment, frustrations, family is a God-given gift. The nurturing, caring, and support that comes from being seen at your worse is God's gift to each of us. It's in these hard times we can really love one another and see the hard times all the way through.

RAISE THEM UP

OVER THE YEARS OF COURTSHIP and planning for their arrival, my queen and I would make such an environment that these two new seeds we created would grow strong and productive. The home is very similar to a greenhouse where spiritual wisdom is grown and cultivated. The power of love, clean living, and strong faith in God is the foundation of family relationships. The home is where the majority of traits for a child's behavior, both good and bad, come from. We understood that our home should be filled with spiritual riches, and both of us must have a servant's spirit. Most family arguments and dissension come from failure to give in to personal rights. One who is filled with the Holy Spirit desires to serve. He or she does not look to establish their own emotional turf but openly encourages others through their spirit.

These are the characteristics and the foundation we would use to bring these angels of God up in this ugly world. As God would have it, I would sustain a serious injury and spend the first nineteen months of their arrival at home with them. I would get to interact in every aspect of this period and remain even until today the proudest father in the world.

As they would grow and enter each phase of childhood, my queen and I would grow even closer. Our family unit was a role model to others on what family and marriage should look like. We would not even entertain separating them to be watched nor would we accept an invite if our jewels could not attend with us.

As they entered preschool and on to elementary school, I would be involved to such a degree where even being the PTA president would become nearly a full-time job for me. Somewhere around their ages of five, I would make a career move to leave the sheriff's office and enter the private sector, and I believe this would become the beginning of the opening of the gates of hell to my family and my life.

CAREER VERSUS GOD

Who Wins?

*L*ET'S LOOK AT THIS IN-DEPTH for a moment before I dive into the makings of my downfall of life. I have had time to process what I will call Work Worshipping. Many workers today are sacrificing themselves on the altar of their careers. They begin to tolerate life-threatening symptoms to include anger, loneliness, chemical dependencies, and many more things in the dead-end pursuit of career success. This so is crazy because many people worship their jobs like it's God himself.

While in my period of what I will call my quiet time (see explanation later on), I found in Psalms 115:4–7 that work is important in the face of true human need. The passage says, "Their idols are silver and gold, made of hands of men. They have mouths, but cannot speak, eyes, but they cannot see; they have ears, but cannot hear, noses but they cannot smell; they have hands, but cannot feel, feet but they cannot walk; nor can they utter a sound with their throats."

This Bible verse is telling us that idols are powerless. And that looking at your work as your idol is just as powerless. In the words of the psalmist, "Those who make them will be like them, and so will all who trust in them" (115:8).

Over my own career, I had seen this happen. I had sat with fellow professionals, powerful and influential men, and watch them cry like babies while they shared their horror stories. Some were personal, others were family, and some even attacks on their characters. At the end of the day, none of their professional accomplishments or their wealth was of any help. They found themselves in trouble and God was no help. I never processed any of these shared stories could ever happen to me. I would later find out that these problems come when we take God's gift of work and begin to worship and serve it rather than Christ.

EXPLANATION OF A FEW ITEMS

*M*Y FATHER WAS A REAL and original black Tony Soprano, and growing up, I saw money as something that came and went and sometimes came in large amounts and sometimes there were periods when it didn't come at all, and during those times, you used what you had saved or back then (what you had put away). I recall my father assisting with my math homework by giving me large amounts of money to count while knowing exactly what he had given me. After counting, he would give a scenario by which I would have to provide the correct change. He would say, "As long as you count your money, you could make it through any math."

WHY DID I STRESS?

*I*N MY LAW ENFORCEMENT CAREER, I taught thousands on how to cope with stress during operations and bad situations. I would explain that the body creates what we would refer to as a chemical cocktail. This mix of chemicals to include adrenaline, endorphins would cause muscles to tighten, tunnel vision, and auditory blockage. This, simply put, was the body freezing and an officer pausing in a bad situation. We called this lag time. During this lag time, the officer would fail to draw their weapon or give a command and in most cases would be injured or even killed. I will use the same basic concept to discuss what happens to us when we stress over things in our lives, and instead of taking action, we wait and react and sometimes it's too late.

There is something called good stress or "eustress," which is from a Latin word that means good. It's not something that is experienced nonstop, but rather creates excitement but then lets the person experiencing it return to a normal state of mind. Bad stress is when our bodies don't return to a normal state and we function in that frozen body state described earlier. This is why we forget things, develop headaches, snap at loved ones, and even become ill.

The bad stress hurts us because it comes from things our minds imagine and we don't take action on. This is the kind of stress that does not go away after an argument with your spouse or disciplining your children or dealing with the person at work who plucked your nerve. It's dangerous and sometimes can even be life threatening. Let's use another example where anxiety affects us. Some people allow their thoughts to control them by focusing on the worst. This is when you stay in response mode. In most cases, this anxiety haunts us in our quiet time, our sleep, or while driving alone.

YOUR ACTIONS WILL ALWAYS
BECOME YOUR BELIEFS

*Y*OU MUST BE WILLING TO change the way you think, and the only way to do that is change your way of thinking. You need to have a positive attitude and will only happen if your faith rest in God. A great motivation speaker, Willie Jolly, says it only takes a minute to change your life!

For years, I would tell officers they only had hundreds of a second to save their lives or the life of someone else because they only had that time to process and make a decision.

While my intention is to not write or speak to my readers and audience like law enforcement, my concept of survival is based on the principles I have taught for years. The concept would become and maintain how I would mortally survive my prison term.

How we deal with stress and anxiety is based on where one's faith lies. I will not say that just because we are Christians, we shouldn't have stress. Actually, I will proffer to you it's the exact opposite. The more you dwell in the word, the more negative things will attack you. Christians must stay in planning mode while creating the positive outcomes they desire. Over time due to many variables—reality television shows, music, negative magazines, and movies. All these vehicles have distorted Christians' thinking and forced us to allow our actions to become what we believe.

HOW DO WE CORRECT THIS?

I FOUND WHILE IN PRISON THAT what got me through was the power of positive thinking. I found that just like my former profession before we entered a bad situation we had tools to use. We had tools to break doors, lights to remove darkness, and many weapons. In prison, I had to build a spiritual tool box, and in it, I put prayer, mediation, positive thoughts, fasting, and as hard as it was, I put clean food in. Each one of these tools was useful in my battle with the fight to maintain my spirit in prison, especially after losing my mother while there. I would like to explain how to use each one in your own situation.

Prayer is how you start a dialogue or conversation with God, and it doesn't take any training or specific language to do it. It's just a touch of honesty and desire to start your relationship with the one who gave his only begotten son for our sins. God is always looking for opportunities to reveal his power to each of us. So starting right now, I challenge you to try. Find a quiet place (just you), and just like you read, begin a dialogue with God. Do not make any assumptions on how the answer will come, but I guarantee you are in for some incredible things to come.

MEDITATION

I FOUND THAT MEDITATION WAS MY grounding to find my inner self. I would sit and ground myself with slow breathing until I was at a mental place where I could begin to sometimes hear my own heartbeat. I would pick a word or place that bought me peace, then focus on that positive energy. I would do this for fifteen to sixty minutes and then pray after. This combination made me almost dangerous to any opposition—a guard with a bad attitude, an ignorant inmate, or sometimes a combination of both.

Positive Thoughts

During and after meditation, I focused on nothing but positive thoughts. I found that what I thought or believed in would become my actions. So when confronted with negative energy, I found something positive to switch to.

Fasting

I learned that fasting was bigger than just removing food, but yet fasting could be fasting from negative words, actions, and food too. I would fast from eating at least two days per month as a minimum, but my fast from any negative language was permanent through my prison term until even now. That's a commitment I made to God that I would keep permanently. I read any positive book, magazine, or paper I could get my hands on to increase my vocabulary to even use good words in place of bad ones.

Clean Eating

Well, in prison, this was a challenge, but I would focus on lots of fish straight out of the package, tuna, mackerel, fruit salads, veggies, and one gallon of water per day. I would shave off twenty-five pounds in my first forty-five days in prison.

This mixture of what was in my tool bag for survival can help you through your relationship problems, straight through school, financial problems, additional struggles, and anything else that's causing your mind to be filled with bad thoughts and beliefs that are making you take bad actions.

The Bible tells us in Proverbs 16:7, "When a man's ways are pleasing to the Lord, he makes even his enemies live at peace with him."

THE TASTE OF MONEY

*O*KAY, SO THE WAY THE rest of this story plays out will be what made you buy this book or will become the reason you come to hear me tell my Why.

So I have laid the foundation for you of how the wrong idol can be tragic. Pay attention as to how my moral compass went off its axis and went to what we call in operations magnetic distortion and drove me into my moral wreck.

When I left the sheriff's office and went to the private sector, it immediately took me away from home which, as you have heard up to now, was my rock. My first piece of work took me to more foreign countries than I can count or even speak of. These trips paid extremely well from what I was used to. Well, money and travel can bring temptation to a man like he has never seen before.

Now this moral breakthrough had begun before I left law enforcement and was partially one of the reasons I left. My wife and I had been initially tested after I went through the process we go through after a fatal shooting. I had befriended a woman who I was comfortable speaking to, and over a period of time, we became closer, and while on my undercover assignment with the FBI, my wife came to me to question the relationship. I admitted that I was wrong, and while we worked through our differences and made amends, I would later fall back and hurt my wife again. Now early on, I spoke of lust and its temporary emotion and long-term pain. This behavior while wrong in the eyes of my relationship was even worse in the eyes of God, and later, you will see the actual cost that I will pay for my actions.

You see, when money and career become what you focus on, you no longer fear God. I could actually sit in front of church and be Mr. Heathcliff Huxtable, with our friends and family and yet betray God and my wife and not even see the wrong in it. Once you forget that your thoughts become your actions, you become dangerous and reckless, especially when the thoughts are negative.

As my business mind and my reputation would grow, so did my ego and my distance away from God. I would become one of the most sought-after security minds for training and protection in the world. Speaking to thousands around the world, I would, after moving through several companies and multiple senior level corporate positions, find myself working for the government as a federal employee and still at the top of the food chain.

MY RISE TO MY MORAL COLLAPSE

*I*N 2007, WHILE IN A government position, I found an opportunity to allow my creative mind to make a mark in history. I would create a tool that would become a standard for my agency to utilize to assist in the protection of tens of thousands of facilities around the country.

Over a period of several years, I would travel, speaking and displaying this methodology to many people and organizations. I would have many opportunities to take private jobs, but my duty to my country made me proud. I would work my way into many senior level working groups with many officials, spend time with congressional staff, White House staff, and leaders from the private sectors as well as law enforcement at all levels. My need for power and ego stroking would continue to grow and would outgrow my position and find it necessary to move to another agency. Now I had heard that a move to this specific agency could be a bad decision, but I always liked a challenge, so I went anyway.

WORKING IN THE JAWS OF THE BEAST

I INITIALLY WENT TO THE OTHER agency to assist them with a major issue where they found themselves spending nearly $30 million on a deliverable that did not work. I used my expertise to create a temporary solution to a problem that had congressional attention. After about ninety days on my detail and pondering my return to my permanent position, an opportunity for a position would open for me to apply to. I would apply and win the position over several other people. Once I was in the position, it took me about two to three weeks to see I was an Oscar swimming in a tank of piranhas and they were going to bite as soon as I would bleed a drop of blood. The main predator would be my direct supervisor who never gave me a solid piece of direction to ensure he always had plausible deniability unless it was something good and he would take the credit. The guy had it in for me so bad, he would publically note my every action regarding my attire and even brand of watch I would wear into a meeting.

BLINDED BY MY OWN SIGHT

I WOULD HAVE NO IDEA I was marked for my own moral disaster upon my arrival. I was so caught up in the job that I missed all the clear signs that I was headed down a road I was not equipped to travel. You see, I was so caught up in the game and my moral compass astray, I had forgotten very basic values learned early in life.

God's instructions are not at all difficult. I must tell you that they are really designed to free us, not lock us into trick bags we find ourselves in. The issue is that we have developed into a culture of "get rich quick" that includes the way we purchase our homes, cars, food, and our clothes. God's principles regarding finances have been ignored in this country for more than fifty years, and now we suffer for it today.

THE COFFEE SHOP DEAL

*Y*OU SEE, IN 2006, I purchased a piece of property and we built a dream home, and after taking a year to construct, we were excited to just move in. So at settlement when the numbers for the mortgage came in nearly $2 thousand over what we expected as a mortgage, we still moved forward and signed and took possession of the home because not only did I not know any better at the time, it was "only" money and I had it.

You see, this is important because what happens next is because I was now a slave to a thing. So a few years later, when an old friend of mine, who I had not spoken to for a few years, called and wanted to discuss business, I was wide open. Now, don't forget I'm still on a journey for power and prestige so I also had aspirations of political office too! So we would meet and after small talk, we would discuss my future in government and my desire to transition to another career in the next two years and run for a public office. We discussed an opportunity with his company, and I would, during this conversation, discuss an opportunity with my agency for his company. Oh no, a deal with the devil has been made.

THE WOLF IN SHEEP'S CLOTHES

*W*ELL, I WOULD HAVE NO idea this meeting was a well-orchestrated plan by my own government I was proud to serve.

Yes, I was now a target of a federal investigation and did not even know it! I would sign a consulting agreement and receive three checks totaling a whole $12,000 and provide him nothing. After three months, a gut feeling felt I should cancel our agreement. But there was no communication from the "friend." After nearly two years and becoming the key to the 2012 inauguration of the second term of Barack Obama, I would be called in for a meeting with investigators.

THE IMPACT OF THE MORAL WRECK

So I respond to the investigator's office under the guise that we would be discussing several cases I had handed over months previous. Once inside the room with investigators, the discussion seemed to focus on issues surrounding my head boss and his ethical misconduct. I could not nor would I agree to choose to discuss his personal business. After a while, the tables turned to me and the same type of questioning and issues, and it was revealed I was the target of the actual interview. I was blown away!

I immediately took full accountability for receiving the checks, and assumed after doing so, I would be given a few days' suspension and a slap on the wrist. Just then, a letter of pre-indictment was given to me, and I was instructed to report to headquarters and surrender my credentials. I was numb inside. I reported to my headquarters where my boss, chief of staff, and others awaited my arrival. After I surrendered my credentials, I was driven home where all my government-issued equipment was also taken away. My wife and son were home and were in complete shock!

WHAT'S NEXT? THEY ASK

*A*FTER EXPLAINING TO MY WIFE and son what had just happened, I had to immediately respond to my lawyer's office to get a handle on what was to come. Once at my lawyer's office, he got a rundown from me and then he called in another lawyer who focused on white-collar crime and was advised of the serious nature of the potential charges pending, and I must say I was scared for the first time in my adult life of the judicial system. After twenty-eight years of upholding the law and only a speeding ticket in 1988, I was now in need of a criminal lawyer. It was like a bad dream.

After the initial legal meeting, they concluded we had to consult another big gun that was based in Baltimore, the former lawyer for my father years ago. So the legal team immediately contacted the prosecution to acknowledge I had counsel and the journey would begin. After about two weeks of extreme stress and anxiety, we got an appointment with the big gun in Baltimore. We met with him and immediately suggested trial, which I was against because I felt I needed to accountable for what I had done. The big gun recommended I consult a lawyer in Virginia who was familiar with the charging district and would be a lot less expensive.

MEETING TO DECIDE NEXT STEPS

$\mathcal{A}$S WE WAITED FOR THE next steps and our appointment with the new lawyer, it seemed as if time just stopped. Once the appointment date came, I went to meet him, and at the last minute, my parents decided to come along for support. We began the sit-down and discussed option versus charges and, of course, fees to take my case. Now during this time, I was in final planning for my two kids to begin school and also working to modify the mortgage on the house. Let me break the full extent of my stress down.

House: We had fought for several years to reduce the note on the house, and it was just that, a fight. I began to fear I would not be able to make the payments at all. Each time, I came down the road and approached our home we lived in, a feeling of fear would overcome me that we could lose our home.

The fear activated the devil. Just like Job, "the thing that I feared came upon me and what I dreaded has happened to me" (Job 3:25). I'm sure Satan was sitting back at this point and with his feet up laughing and eating popcorn because I was emotionally spinning out of control. I was processing:

- Kids going to school
- Going to jail
- Not having my home
- Would my marriage survive all
- Public and family disappointment

As time would progress and my lawyer would work with prosecutor, I resigned from my position, hoping it would ease the blow, but after resigning, they continued the full court press, seeking the maximum within their power with no real hope of giving me a fair shot. At some point, I began to work, delivering medical supplies between Maryland, Washington, DC, Virginia, and Delaware 24/7, 365. I also got a small consulting gig with a security vendor to assist on a few administrative issues they had. In April, I would stand before a federal judge and take a plea deal to one count of conspiracy and get a sentence date nearly two months away.

I recall that plea being sometime around 10:00 a.m., and by the time we were done and processed by the US marshals and released on personal recognizance, it was about noon. My wife and I exited the courthouse and walked about 150 yards to a sandwich shop and my phone was blowing up that it was all over the news, to include national news affiliates. I knew we had to get to my kids and in-laws before they got hit with media rumors. We sat the kids down and explained next steps. I explained I would be putting the house on the market and downsizing and preparing for worst-case scenario. The kids and in-laws seemed understanding, but it was still a big pill to chew. Over the next few months, I would use every waking moment to prepare us for the journey ahead.

GRABBING MY DEMONS BY THE HORNS

A MAN WHO HARBORS UNFORGIVENESS WILL never win. No matter how wrong he or his adversary is. Refusing to forgive means accepting corruption in life, and that corruption begins in your relationship with God and affects all your other relationships.

I decided on a Sunday during church to let the Holy Spirit to use me and give my testimony to my church family and in the presence of my wife and kids. When I stood in front of my church congregation, I had an out-of-body experience and spirit had me provide a full testimony to include my indiscretions with my wife years prior. After asking God for forgiveness and I must tell you that after the spirit let the words out, I felt my burdens leave my heart as the Lord took them as his own. My wife and children came to embrace me as they said they loved me and would be by my side as a family through the storm. I was greeted after church by my entire church family who said they would be there for us every step of the way. Many said they were inspired and, because of my testimony, would change some things in their lives.

NOW WE WAIT

HE WAIT BETWEEN TAKING MY plea and my sentence day was about ninety days, and I can tell you, it was the longest ninety days of my life. I learned to wait on God is a struggle and will result in failure. I believe failure is where we learn success. Failure teaches us to wait by God's mercy instead of waiting on his mercy. So the very one thing we wait for is the only thing we should wait by! Our strength is never going to be what sees us through a season, but rather God's mercy.

I would lose all my work as a consultant with the two security companies due to my media play on my circumstance, so now, I would have to live off my savings and begin to lower our standard of living to allow savings to carry us through.

It would be during this time I find out who my real friends and family were because I was now in my darkest hour, and to my surprise, many people stayed away or gave many excuses why they couldn't come around. There will be some family and former friends who read this and experience this journey for the first time because they stayed away. After a while, you grow numb to rumors or losing your home or how much time you will get and you just rely on God.

I had never heard so many excuses from people in my life. It was during this time I would meet a young professional black woman who would introduce me and my wife to a business that had a network marketing drive to it and came across as the most positive group of people I had ever met, and this kept my focus on positive thoughts at least for a while. It lasted for a few months until the magnitude of my situation was a bit much for her to monitor, and she began to struggle with the magnitude of my burden, but she would she would remain a good friend even to today. The positive energy I did carry away from that experience forced me to read some incredible books and videos and stay focused on positivity.

As we waited for sentencing, my mother began to have various doctor appointments surrounding her second battle with cancer and I would attend with her since I was no longer working full-time. We would enjoy this quality time together and just talk, sometimes eat lunch or just enjoy a smoothie together at her favorite smoothie place.

MY HARDSHIP STILL HAD NOT BEGUN YET

*A*S TIME WOULD PROGRESS AND sentencing would grow close, it seemed as if my preparation, both administrative and spiritual, would require more and more time and resources, and yet still many people said they were there. However, only a small group of four to five maximum would step up.

As I searched my Bible for answers to the many questions I had, I would start at the beginning to the book of Genesis. I could not help but notice how God seemed to connect with us as people. It seems at first God stayed close when he walked in the garden with them on a direct speaking level and punished them directly. Even when Abraham's time came, he sent messages out on door-to-door calls. By Jacob's time, the messages would change to more unclear; there were dreams about ladders and weird things. Then toward the end, a guy named Joseph gets direction in an unimaginable way. Here is where I note the book slows down. It begins to show God working behind the scenes. It seems if anyone would be upset with God, it should have been Joseph, who even though he tried to do right, trouble still came to him. He told his own brothers about a dream and they punished him. He ran from a married woman who tried to throw herself on him and he still was put in jail. Then while in prison helped his cell mate out, he forgot about them. I tell you because like Joseph may have done, I asked God was he being unfair. Then I went back to my relationship with my mother and shifted to her as a seasoned parent. I now see that God pulled her away from me, like he had Joseph, to allow our faith to reach the next level. I believe through Joseph's trials, Joseph learned to trust as should I. Genesis

50:20 says, "You intended it for good…" I believe this scripture told me that there were some who wanted me destroyed, but God had good intentions for me in all that was going on.

JUDGMENT DAY

$\mathcal{M}$Y SENTENCE DAY WOULD COME and my support from church family and a few select family and friends would be incredible. I would hear the prosecutor and judge speak of me like a hard calculating criminal as I would await my moment to speak. During my short moment, I would turn to my family and again apologize for my actions and beg for their forgiveness. I would then redirect myself to the judge and again apologize to both the judge and the court, my country and the state that I would accept my punishment as God's will being done and that I only pray that I could see my kids off to school in a few weeks. The judge would find it to allow me to do so and then made a decision to impose a fifteen-month prison sentence upon me. The prosecutor appeared very disappointed as he wanted his victory to be to completely destroy me.

I was numb to hear a prison sentence handed down and it be directed at me! After sentencing, I was processed again by various special agents and marshals and later released. I would greet those outside who stood in support and thank them and then return home to sit down with my kids. Over the next few weeks, we would secure a new residence and downsize in preparation as the bank was not willing to modify the loan and left no other option than to file bankruptcy.

LOAD GETS HEAVIER

$\mathcal{A}$S WE BEGIN OUR MOVE process after seven years in 7,000 square feet of house (Humble 7) (expound on biblical 7) with limited help, limited budget, and summer heat. We as a family of four and help from my sister-in-law and siblings get the bulk of it ready for movers who would come on two dates to work around my budget.

On a Friday afternoon, my sister would call me to advise me my mother had just suffered a heart attack and headed into surgery. I made it to the hospital in record time to be with my family. Once at the hospital, I would be told her condition was stable, and there was a minor complication with the stent in her leg, but she would make it through. She would be admitted and stayed for several days. My family and I would work together in two-people shifts and never leave her side. After several days of up and down moments between a major back pain issue and the heart attack, she was to be discharged on Tuesday. Before her discharge, my sister, who is in the hospital staff circle, shared a family concern about my mother's speech and memory, and a CAT scan was ordered.

A few hours later, the attending physician would enter the room where my youngest sister, a church leader, my daughter, and I were all with my mother and gave words I will never forget. He said, "I hate news like this, but the brain is full of cancer."

It was like time stopped. As the family would all come together immediately, we began major prayer sessions, and over the next few days, we would find out the cancer had filled her lungs too. The doctors would order immediate treatment to begin the following week which was three weeks away from self-report date. I would attend every single appointment with her, and while she would try and keep that big smile like only the sun can shine, the pain sometimes would get the best of her. I would continue to be by her side daily until the day I would depart for self-report to federal prison.

REPORTING TO SERVE IN A NEW WAY

ON SEPTEMBER 4, 2013, I would hit the road to begin my prison sentence. I would stop to see my mother to take her infectious smile and energy with me. My good friend who is very private and reserved and a cousin would take me up the night before so I could stay in a hotel and get a good night's sleep. We left my parents' home and hit the road. Once in New Jersey, we stopped to eat what was called my last supper of the free world. After eating my meal, we went to my hotel, and after a few short jokes and handshakes and hugs, they would leave and I would be left to process my day and fifteen-month journey ahead. The front desk attendant would notice that I was using points for my stay instead of standard payment, and once she saw I was a platinum guest who was on his way to prison, she offered me the best room in the hotel. After calling my wife from the front desk, I would attempt to relax and reflect on the events prior to this night and then try to process the months to come. I took thirty- to forty-five-minute naps through the night as my thoughts of prison and the feeling of abandonment to my family, and I couldn't help but wonder if I would ever see my mother again.

THE DAY OF HUMILITY ARRIVES

SEPTEMBER 4, 2013, WOULD BE the day I dreaded for about six months. As the morning came, it was as if I was numb and the feeling of a dead calm was over me. I tried to eat, but my stomach and nerves were completely out of control. I recall I was able to get some tea down and that was it. A part of me even felt like leaving the hotel room I only slept in for only a night was home, and I felt attached to it. When I came down, my sedan would be waiting, and the feeling of even getting into it was weird as it seemed to have a destination of gloom and doom.

I climbed in and off I went. The seven-mile ride seemed like an eternity, and I preferred not to speak even as the driver wanted to be polite. After the short ride of eternity and we pulled onto federal property, I began to feel the walls come in around me. As we break the corner into a compound, I see what appears to be a maximum security looking penitentiary, we pull in and I recall the driver saying we are here and my body was stiff. I couldn't feel my body move at all, nor could I really process the sight of me going in to that place.

I would exit the car and walk toward the entrance, and in seconds, I was approached by a small marked federal prison vehicle driven by a heavily armed federal guard. I recall him saying, "Are you self-reporting?"

I said, "Yes, sir."

He called into the facility on his radio and said, "You got one coming in."

He asked to see my reporting document and asked what property I had. I advised that I had my Bible and cash for my commissary deposit. He advised no one would be able to take cash today. Now

I had been clearly told to bring only cash, so I was taken back. He advised since it was only 10:00 a.m. and I had until noon, I could go to Western Union myself the money, and he gave me my inmate number. I requested to the driver to take me to the closest Western Union. After sending the money, I came back.

NOT THE KIND OF WELCOME YOU LOOK FOR

$\mathcal{A}$s I entered the first door and it shut, *bang*. I recall going through a metal detector and about six large steel doors, it felt like the death march. Once inside, I was taken into a room and told, not asked, to remove all articles of clothing, and then lift my genitals and cough, then turn around and spread my butt cheeks and cough again. This was the most degrading thing I had to ever do in my life. Now, for years as a law enforcement officer, I had seen this from the other side, but today, the tables had turned. Next, I would be DNA tested again as if the other three times by agents in federal lockup was not enough, I was fingerprinted, photographed, TB tested, and evaluated by a doctor. After all this, I would be placed in a steel and concrete cell where I would sit for hours like a forgotten animal. Interestingly enough, I was allowed to keep my prescriptions, so I took a few of them to calm my anxiety and relax. Now for hours, I could only process the next year in a cell like this and asking myself, "How in hell am I going to do this?" After a few hours of walking a thin line of peace and insanity, the doors opened and I was asked to stand up and walk with the guards.

They walked me back to the same entry doors I walked in, and I was confused because we were headed back outside and I was not cuffed or shackled at all. Once we got to the door, I was told to walk the sidewalk and proceed across the parking lot to a small group of double wide trailers. I recall being very hesitant to follow instructions because it felt like a setup. It was as if I was being allowed to walk far enough to be shot for escaping. I quickly realized now I was walking over to what was called low or camp side. This is where I would serve my time and not in the Max Unit.

TIME TO COPE WITH DOING TIME

I ENTERED THE FACILITY AND WAS directed to a man in an office where I would have the worst introduction to a person you could ever imagine.

This man was maybe the unhappiest adult I have ever met in my adult life. As he gave me his speech of dos and don'ts using the F-bomb too many times to count, he dismissed me. I asked him before I left if I could share a letter of prognosis from my mother's doctor regarding her cancer. He responded with, "I don't give a fuck about your mother being ill or dying. People fucking die when you're fucking locked, locked up, so deal with it!"

When he was done, I very tactfully asked could I be excused. I needed to leave because it was best. He had no idea how angry I was becoming from the disrespect he had just shown to me.

LETTING NEGATIVE THOUGHTS GO!

*A*s I began my prison term, I quickly learned I had to find myself a moral out. That meant finding a way to not allow the many negative and unhealthy thoughts I was thinking control my actions. Believe me, I had thoughts of anger toward the former friend who brought this prison opportunity to my doorstep. I would actually be listening to another inmate talk to me sometime and really not be listening, but rather processing how bad I would physically destroy them if there were ever a need to do so. I initially despised all officers who did not speak to me with respect and processed my punishment if I said what I thought. Anyone of non-color who seemed they were the slightest bit racist I checked and made sure they knew I was not going to be the least bit willing to engage in any conversation with.

Then about a full week into my prison sentence as I searched my Bible for answers, God directed me to a verse that read: "Do not let this book of law depart your mouth; meditate on it day and night, so that you may be careful to do everything written in it." After reading this one verse, I quickly realized that for most of my adult life, I had never really processed how damaging my own thoughts had actually been. It became so clear to me that Satan had been filling my head with lies and garbage that had wasted years of my time. All this was because he was controlling my thoughts. I began to accept that all my adult indiscretions to include my going to prison were based on my thoughts becoming my actions. While spending time in a federal prison was an experience within itself I will not speak to much on my full experience in this first book because like the other experiences in my life, it does not define who I am or became. I also refuse to allow the system too much ink or time in my rebuilding of my life.

This would go from clear to crystal clear when I found another scripture.

"As for you, you were dead in your transgressions and sins, in which you used to live when you followed the ways of the world and of the ruler of the kingdom of the air, the spirit who is now at work in those who are disobedient" (Ephesians 2:1-3).

Now, this verse from this book hit me like a brick against my head because the book was written by Apostle Paul who wrote the letter from prison. In the second half of his letter, he writes about living life as a Christian.

CLEAR YOUR MIND FOR A NEW YOU

*A*s I CONTINUE MY DESIRE to open your understanding as to how my story may assist you during your journey, let me speak on how my mind clearing and way of changing my thought mattered. I will stay with the Apostle Paul for a while.

Paul writes: "Do not conform any longer to the pattern of this world, but be transformed by renewing of your mind then you will be able to test and approve what God's will is—his good, pleasing and perfect will" (Romans 12:2).

This passage would become the game changer for me because I had been trying to process how to deal with a new lifestyle while in prison, my mother fighting on her death bed, abandoning my wife and kids, wondering if my kids could handle the pressure, wondering if my wife would weather the storm, wondering if I would snap and hurt someone in prison, wondering who would write or visit me. These were just a few of the things that I processed daily.

At the end of the day, I began to realize that in order for me to stay in the fight and go the whole fifteen rounds of that heavyweight championship was to clear my mind and circle around me of all negativity and stay positive.

WHEN GOD GIVES THE SILENT TREATMENT

*N*OW PLEASE DON'T MISUNDERSTAND THAT when I wrote this, I always had a 100 percent positive attitude because believe me, I didn't. Not only was I in prison, but I had things around me that were the epitome of negative. There were times I would stop and pray to God and there would be complete 100 percent "silence." I would give an explanation of the silence I speak of in the twenty-second division of Psalms:

"My God, my God, why have you forsaken me? Why are you so far from saving me, so far from my cries of anguish? My God, I cry out by day, but you do not answer, by night, but I find no rest. Yet you are enthroned as the Holy One; you are the one Israel praises. In you our ancestors put their trust; they trusted and you delivered them. To you they cried out and were saved; in you they trusted and were not put to shame. But I am a worm and not a man, scorned by everyone, despised by the people. All who see me mock me; they hurl insults, shaking their heads. 'He trusts in the Lord,' they say, 'let the Lord rescue him. Let him deliver him, since he delights in him.' Yet you brought me out of the womb; you made me trust in you, even at my mother's breast. From birth I was cast upon you; from my mother's womb you have been my God. Do not be far from me, for trouble is near and there is no one to help. Many bulls surround me; strong bulls of Bashan encircle me. Roaring lions that tear their prey open their mouths wide against me. I am poured out like water, and all my bones are out of joint. My heart has turned to wax; it has melted within me. My mouth is dried up like a potsherd, and my tongue sticks to the roof of my mouth; you lay me in the dust of death. Dogs surround me, a pack of villains encircles me; they pierce my hands and my feet. All my bones are on display; people stare and gloat over me.

They divide my cloths among them and cast lots for my garment. But you, Lord, do not be far from me. You are my strength; come quickly to help me. Deliver me from the sword, my previous life from the power of the dogs. Rescue me from the mouth of the lions; save me from the horns of the wild oxen. I will declare your name to my people; in the assembly I will praise you. You who fear the Lord, praise him! All you descendants of Jacob, honor him! Revere him, all you descendants of Israel! For he has not despised or scorned the suffering of the afflicted one; he has not hidden his face from him but has listened to his cry for help. From you comes the theme of my praise in the great assembly; before those who fear you I will fulfill my vows. The poor will eat and be satisfied; those who seek the Lord will praise him—may your hearts live forever! All the ends of the earth will remember and turn to the Lord, and all the families of the nations will bow down before him, for dominion belongs to the Lord and he rules over the nations. All the rich of the earth will feast and worship; all who go down to the dust will kneel before him—those who cannot keep themselves alive. Posterity will serve him; future generations will be told about the Lord. They will proclaim his righteousness, declaring to a people yet unborn: He has done it!"

It was here I would learn to understand I needed to be worried and bent out of shape for what had not come to me yet, but rather look at what God had already done for me. As I began to meditate and pray on those things, it would force me to thank God, and immediately, I would be forced to thank God for what I had or had already been blessed with. Then my positive thinking would kick back in.

A great example of this was when I was in the early stages of my sentence. I would get very upset at family and friends, specifically my wife for not visiting me as much as I would have liked. And on a couple of occasions, my wife would tell me often how busy she was running around for our children after work and weekends. I recall a couple of instances where her comments upset me so bad I came close to asking her not to bother to come back to visit me at all the rest of my time in prison. I was focused on what I wanted in seeing her and the kids instead of being grateful she didn't leave me and had come to see me before and that God had let her and the kids make it home safely.

The more I prayed on this Psalm and its meaning, the more I began to hear God's word in my heart and the negative energy would leave my spirit.

LIVING MY BEST WHILE IN EXILE

I FOUND MYSELF EXILED AND LIVING with an element I despised my entire life: thugs, knocking heads, and drug dealers. This was going to be interesting.

I would ask myself, "Should I sit and feel sorry for myself or focus positive energy or making the best of this bad situation?"

Each one of us has faced what I will call exile times in our lives—loss of job, loss of loved one, broken relationships, and separation from church. These days, months, years, or however long these periods last are the times we wish we were somewhere else in our lives. These times let us know what is really important in our lives and help us see those things that really matter to us and what makes us look to the Lord with all we have.

"This is what the Lord Almighty, the God of Israel, says to all those I carried into exile from Jerusalem to Babylon. 'Build houses and settle down; plant gardens and eat what they produce. Marry and have sons and daughters; find wives for your sons and give your daughters in marriage, so that they too may have sons and daughters. Increase in number there; do not decrease. Also, seek the peace and prosperity of the city to which I have carried you into exile. Pray to the Lord for it, because if it prospers, you too will prosper.' Yes, this is what the Lord Almighty; the God of Israel, says. 'Do not let the prophets and diviners among you deceive you. Do not listen to the dreams you encourage them to have. They are prophesying lies to you in my name. I have not sent them,' declares the Lord. This is what the Lord says: 'When seventy years are completed for Babylon, I will come to you and fulfill my good promise to bring you back to this place. For I know the plans I have for you,' declares the Lord, 'plans to prosper you and not to harm you, plans to give you hope and a

future. Then you will call on me and come and pray to me, and I will listen to you. You will seek me and find me when you seek me with all your heart. I will be found by you,' declares the Lord, 'and will bring you back from captivity.' I will gather you from all the nations and places where I have banished you,' declares the Lord, 'and will bring you back to the place from which I carried you into exile'" (Jeremiah 29:4–14).

ACTUAL JOURNAL ENTRY

In Exile and Living Out Our Real Potential
(9/19/2013)

I HAVE FOUND IN MY STAY here in federal prison while living in what feels like a life of exile (being where we don't want to be with people we don't want to be with) forces a decision: Will I focus my attention on what is wrong with this place or even what's wrong with this world and feel sorry for myself? Or will I focus my energies on how I can live at my best in this place I find myself? It is always easier to complain about problems than to engage them.

During both in prison and life, we face decisions on how we will respond to these exile conditions. We can say, "I don't like it. I want to be where I was ten years ago."

How can you expect me to throw myself into what I don't like—that would be sheer hypocrisy. What sense is there in taking risks and tiring myself out among people I don't even like in a place where each day there is feeling of having no future.

Or we can say: "I will do my best with whatever I find here. Far more important than the climate of this place is the God of this place. God is here with me."

What I am experiencing right now is on the ground that was created by him and with people whom he still loves. It is just as possible to live out God's will here as any place else. I came in here full of anxiety. I didn't know my way around. I had a lot to learn, but couldn't show it. Sometimes, I thought of not making it. Change is hard. Developing intimacy among strangers is always a risk. Building relationships in unfamiliar and borderline hostile surroundings is difficult. But if that is what it means to be alive, human, then I will do it.

All of us are given moments, even days, months, years of exile. What will you do with them? Wish we were someplace else? Complain? Escape into fantasies? Drug ourselves into oblivion? Or will we build and plant a seed in a peaceful mind-set we inhabit and people we are around? Exile reveals what really matters and frees us to pursue what really matters, which is to seek the Lord with all our hearts.

ACTUAL JOURNAL ENTRY

My Letter to Heaven

HELLO, GOD,

I pray this letter finds you in midst of the productions of more miracles for mankind. I know we speak on a regular basis, but today, I find the need to write you a letter. First, I want to say congratulations to you on your new arrival of one of your greatest creations, yes, God, my mother. I know she was your child and yours to bring home when you were ready, but God I would like to discuss a few things with you just for me to have some clarity. The first big question, I will just cut to the chase and ask, Am I ready for her to be gone? God, you brought me to prison and separated me from my family and took my mother away so she could be closer to you. I'm just trying to better understand your timing. I am not questioning your decision, but rather asking do you intend to let me know how to deal with the many, many emotions I feel? You know I do have anger, while it's not all directed at you, I do have it. As you know I feel lonely, abandoned, guilty, sad, scared, and maybe even depressed just to name a few. Of course, you know exactly everything I feel because you are God! LOL. Sorry, had to make myself laugh to keep writing.

God, as I search my Bible for answers before writing to you and taking time away from my mother, I found lots of scripture where most likely you sent me anyway! I won't quote them all, but when you say in the book of Joel 2:32, "And everyone who calls on your name will be saved; for on Mount Zion and in Jerusalem there will be deliverance, as you said, among the survivors whom you call."

Okay, God, I very much as David, called upon and confessed my sins! Can I assume since I can't have any more children that you took my mother instead? That's a question. Now, God, I clearly understand that you will answer me when you're ready in whatever way you choose. Okay, next question. Did you have to make my mother suffer before you brought her home? Was that for her to see if she would curse you? Like you tested Job? Or was that for those of us you left here in this cruel world?

Okay, I don't mean to sound as if I have a tone, but you know, I have not been able to discuss this with anyone except you and your oldest son, Jesus, who you know is my closest friend, next to you. LOL

Okay, no more jokes! I recall in the book of Matthew 17:20 you said, "Faith only the size of a mustard seed would allow a mountain to move." Lord, if you needed to test my faith, was taking me away from my family and nearly all my earthly possessions not enough that you needed to take my mother too?

Okay, I know you hear tone again! Lord, this is hard for me, so please allow me to speak from my heart because it really hurts right now.

Okay, now you have just had me pause and look at the book of Luke, and yes, I see 7:28 and your son Jesus. "I tell you, among those born of women there is no one greater than John; yet the one is least in the kingdom of God is greater than he." Did you send me to that as a comparison of me and mother as mom and son and then me to John? God, I'm trying.

Okay, I believe now you have the Holy Spirit sitting with me because I just went to Romans 14:8 where you say or rather Paul says, "If we live, we live to you. So whether we live or die, we belong to you." So I'm guessing you took me there to show me because my mother lived her life to you at its fullest, you took her because you said you would! I get that, but my big question is still not yet clear. Was I or am I ready? Okay, I know I said I was not going to tell you what your own book says, but in case, others hear of this letter, I wanted to have them understand our conversation. I just found in 1 Corinthians 15:57, "But thanks be to you; you give us the victory through your son Jesus Christ."

I can only assume you are still telling me that while I'm in prison and all I feel, you have already forgiven me when you sent your son to die on the cross, and that you took my mother away because her work here was done, and the only way to get her home close to you was to make her absent of the earthly body I knew! I get it!

I guess you just had me look at the book of Malachi where Malachi prophesies during deplorable conditions described in Nehemiah 13. Calling on those complacent in their spiritual life to renew our relationship with you and that you promised blessings to those of us who did it. As I read the book, I promise you not to be complacent in my faith, and ensure I put your will before my own concerns. I see in 4:2 it reads, "But for you who revere my name, the sun of righteousness will rise with healing in its wings, and you will go out and leap like calves released from the stall."

God, I believe I received the bulk of my answers tonight in our short conversations, but I would like to keep the door open to further our discussions until at least I'm there sitting with my mother.

God, I know even Jesus wept when Mary went to him and he stood before the tomb (John 11:35). God, I love you, your son, my mother, family, and all your children, but how do I cry in this place where you have placed me?

God, I know you love me and I love you too. Amen.

God, I had to come back. Your answers were received to ensure that when I share your clarity I am able to let others understand it as I do now.

Brothers/Sisters,

I believe I, along with some of you, have misunderstood some writings of Paul when he wrote to his friends in Thessalonica when it says, "We do not want you to be ignorant about those who fall asleep, or to grieve like the rest of men, who have no hope" (1 Thessalonians 4:13). Unfortunately, some of us struggle under grief because we left off the last phrase of the sentence and have missed Paul's point completely.

Paul does not say we are not to grieve. I have learned grief is an emotion like love, fear, guilt, or anger and probably a mixture of all of these. Religion does not make us immune from or to emotion, and it is as pointless to deny grief, but should grieve with hope. Our assurance of resurrection and the trust in God's power to turn bad Tuesdays into good Tuesdays and keep grief from overwhelming us. I don't believe God gives a crown to those who refuse to weep. So yes, big boys cry too. Amen.

WHILE IN PRISON WAS IT REALLY DEPRESSION?

*F*IRST, WAS I DEPRESSED? WELL, I don't know because to admit it would mean I could wind up in solitary confinement.

I believe most people who say they are miserable or depressed are not even aware that their unhappy state or mind is from the vacuum that sucks the God right out of them, and the vacuum is located within themselves. This lack of spirituality or void of God makes them vulnerable to many mental, emotional, and physical disorders. Whether they don't believe in God or just refuse his presence in their lives, it doesn't matter. They experience an empty hunger within themselves for God. But they lack the spiritual resources to help them cope with the problems caused by their ego-driven decisions. This void I speak of dates back as old as man. The Bible calls it death back to the book of Genesis when Adam and Eve disobeyed God, they died spiritually.

When God places a promise in your heart, you have to get yourself to a place where you believe it is going to happen so strongly that no one or any situation can change your mind. It may even seem impossible. All circumstances may tell you that it is not going to happen, but deep down, you have to have this confidence, this knowing, that God is in charge.

God is bigger than any obstacle we may face. He already has made a way for us, and at the right time, what he promises us will come to pass. We must know God is fighting our battles and organizing things in our best interest and making a way even when we don't see a way.

So I want you to do what I did and learn to stop being discouraged and get up in the morning and thank God that the answer is on its way. Instead of talking about how big the problem is, start going through the day talking about how big God is.

Set your mind in one direction: victory, favor, restoration, healing. Sometimes, it may even appear it's taking a long time, but he didn't bring us this far to leave us.

I found while in prison that in times of stress and uncertainty, it is imperative that your faith be strong and focus intact. "You must rely on me when things seem to be out of your control, says the Lord. Nothing is impossible with me, and you can do all that is necessary when you put your trust in me. Be steadfast! I can do all things through Christ who strengthens me" (Philippians 4:13).

ACTUAL JOURNAL ENTRY

9/27/2013

I WAS JUST INFORMED THAT UNDER no circumstances, minus a pardon from the president, will I be allowed out to attend my mother's services. So be it, the devil wins his battle over me, and I wind up in solitary confinement. I wrote the words to follow to be read when the time comes. I want whoever reads it to stand tall, shoulders high, and speak to be heard.

Thank you.

To be read at my mother's funeral service:

A Mother's Unselfish Love

Mom, I write this letter today with a heart as heavy as a man's heart could ever be. As I sit here in prison much like men whom I have written letters from prison before me, I think of men like Paul, John, Dr. King, and Nelson Mandela. What we all share is that we had a mother and a belief in God.

I believe a mother's love is the most unselfish of all love, a love like no other on earth. She has unselfish love for her children, grand-children, family, home, and even work. She is a woman who takes great pride in whatever she sets her mind to do. A real mother will do whatever it takes to make sure her family has a roof over their heads, food to feed them, clothes on their backs, and an education. A real mother will always be here for you, whether it's to lend an ear, or to give you sound advice whether you want to hear it or not. She will also be there for you physically, spiritually, and emotionally! She will have your back 100 percent, 24/7, 365 when no one else will! No matter what! Unselfishly.

A real mother will instill in you principles, morals, values, good work ethics, and prepare you for family and having kids of your own. A real mother will believe in you, encourage you, and inspire you to do well and excel in whatever you pursue, and for you to believe, encourage, and inspire your children and others to do the same! One of the things a real mother wants most of all, is for everyone to get along, love and support one another!

A real mother is not just a mother; she is an extraordinary woman, mother, grandmother, wife, confidant, Delta sister, Eastern Star sister, pastor, business owner, and anything else she chooses, who will love all unselfishly, no matter what!

Mom, I had a real mother, who was all the above! Mom, this was written from my heart and dedicated to you and inspired by you! Mom, we will all miss you, and will forever always love you and cherish you eternally within our hearts! Unselfishly!

So to all of you who came today, I beg you to love your mother, value your mother, cherish your mother, appreciate your mother, and honor your mother, always! Unselfishly!

She deserves nothing less!

Suga

ACTUAL JOURNAL ENTRY

10/9/2013

MY WORDS AFTER RETURNING TO a cell to be stripped, piss tested, and processed after burying my mother!

As I sit in prison twenty-four hours after my mother's funeral, I ask myself, "Does death have the final say?"

I do not believe it does because I found in 1 Corinthians 15:26 it's the last enemy to be destroyed. Jesus is where all my hope must rest to get me through this. He cursed death in his resurrection (15:54-47), and I find my comfort, looking forward to the day when I don't have to say good-bye again.

I believe a good cry might be healthy, but in my current environment, that's not an option for me. So I try and find comfort in writing and searching for my answers in the Bible.

I have heard that it's healthy to feel the way I do, but I usually hear that you should talk about how you feel to, and yet again, I don't have that luxury here in prison. I feel various things to include pain, shock, anger, fear, loneliness, anxiety, and again maybe even depression and yet I must cope with this internally. I believe I will write a letter to God to tell him how I feel.

LETTER TO HEAVEN TO MOM

November 1, 2013

EAR MOM,

As I sit here with you on my mind, I can't help but wonder what you do all day in heaven. I sometimes wonder if you read all day, but I wonder if you did read, what books even are kept in such a magnificent place. I could imagine you relax by the crystal-clear water with your mom and dad and walk among the greatest people to ever walk the earth.

I listen to you daily when you say, "Suga, you can do this." But, Mom, this is so hard for me to bear knowing how bad my father and siblings are hurting. I thought I would write today because a few weeks ago, when you left to go home, I asked God for help and he had me write to him for guidance, and as I wrote the letter, he led me to scripture to find my answers. I ask that you do the same right now. Mom, I want to cry out to you so bad, but I just can't find the place and time in this place. Mom, I need you to show me the way.

When I wrote to God the day of your magnificent Home-Going Service, I told him I was filled with many, many emotions. Mom, I realize how much our relationship meant to me even more now that you're gone. I also see so much clearer it is that I am so much like you that it's incredible. I love and want to help so many people I sometimes forget myself. The other day, when you told me to distance myself from these false teachers around me, you could not have been any clearer. Mom, I thank you for that. I also thank you for reminding me how much I need Carla on my life and that I must stay focused on my love for her. Mom, remember the lady who told us in 1986 I would marry a teacher? And wow, God gave me the best he had! She has kept me grounded from day 1 to now. Mom, I have heard it said that men find wives who have characteristics of their mother's. Well, Mom, Carla's heart is warm, kind, and full of love and peace, just like yours. Please tell God that when I told him that she will be my priority after this journey I meant it!

Hey, I'm sure you were sitting in God's right hand when the DS made the comment about me working at the conference center. When you get some time between helping with miracles, can you send me a sign as to what that really means? Thank you, Mom.

YOUR GOING-HOME SERVICE

*M*OM, I RECALL OUR CONVERSATIONS about going home and what your wishes were. Wow, did Broadneck Church knock it out the park or what?

Mom, I was so proud of Carrie for taking charge and how they all came together. It was a perfect day even in my struggle of knowing it was for you.

Okay, I have to let you know you knocked me out when you walked the warden to me the day after you left. I was blown away because the word was that he was not only a hard a———, but even an atheist. What did you do to pull that off?

I also have questions about the shooting stars the night before you went home. Was that the other angels on their way to get you? After I was done speaking that Tuesday and knew you would leave the next day, I was at peace with you going home. Mom, I am so proud of you and what you accomplished here for your short time here!

I won't keep writing today, but rather save some for prayer tonight. As you can see, my eyes are getting watery and people have come in here, and still, I don't want to let it out. I would like you to tell me how to handle my father and brothers, knowing they are really going through it. The girls seem well, and, Mom, they are so you in their ways and looks. It's like seeing them last week was really like sitting with you. Carrie's funny spirit and big heart are beautiful, and Eshe has the same technique and wit you had here.

Okay, Mom, please continue to watch over me, and if you don't mind, can you touch the judge and have her find a place in her heart to get me home to be by my father and family?

Mom, I love you with all my heart and please continue to walk close to me and show me the right way.

I love you.

OUR PLAYBOOK FOR PRAYER

*G*OOD MORNING TO YOU ALL!

While during my time away in prison, I had many, many hours and days of time to reflect, and during that time of reflection, I observed many religions and ethnic groups of people go about their own display of whom they believed or looked up to in their spiritual journeys. At some point, I became so curious that I began to ask and even worship with a few to find some answers, not to any specific questions I had, but rather just a peek behind the scenes. I mean, we had some players in there too. Stemming from Catholics to Jews, Moores Science Temple, 3 percenters, Muslims, Buddhism, Native Indian, Atheist, Arabic nation, and some I had not even heard of. Wicca, who basically worship Satan!

I guess what I did want to find was some common ground on how I was able to be respected and, in some cases, even feared by each group of people, yet some of these groups hated each other.

So I prayed on it, and God said, "Go and seek your answer."

Well, folks, believe it or not, just that fast my answer was in the very start. As I prayed, I quickly realized everyone prayed to God not even realizing or in some cases admitting it! Truth is, some folks just had a different name for God, that's all.

Now I prayed a lot while in prison. I mean more than I did before going, I remained in prayer mode. I avoided trouble at all cost.

After a month or two of worshiping with the Jews, I began to take issue with their handing over Jesus for crucifixion and their high priest being so unjust to him. They didn't seem to take their worship seriously to me.

The Muslim brothers I found very interesting as they split between the Suni and the Nation brothers. Each stopped and prayed three to five times per day in a full ritual. This intrigued me because I would pray to God while walking on the rec, yard, gym, my bunk, my knees, shower, and anywhere else I felt the urge.

As I searched and researched, I found the Bible does not give an exact time or length for prayer, but it does offer some guidelines. In Psalm 88, prayer is offered in the early morning (V.13), and in Psalm 55, prayers are said evening, morning, and noon (V.17). The psalmist of Psalm 119 even says prayer seven times a day (V.164). Daniel knelt for prayer three times per day (Daniel 6:10). Jesus prayed before sunrise (Mark 1:35) and in the evening when the day's work was over (Mark 6:46). Peter prays at the third, sixth, and ninth hours.

A BRIGHT DARK CHRISTMAS

*I*F YOU CARE ANYTHING ABOUT Christmas, it should mean the beginning and the end. It's a time of darkness and also a light that only few can see or even explain. My Christmas season 2013 was spent sitting in a federal prison, and I tried to put some things in proper perspective. First, I sat in meditation on the first snow day on December 8, 2013, and visualized how and where the birth took place.

Here in my vision was the son of all mankind, the maker of the universe, and he was being born in a stable filled with the smell of horse manure and only God knows what! This seems cruel to any baby and couple to be in this position, but here was the Son of Man, our future coming into this ugly world in such a dark and gloomy place only to become the light of the world!

So as I sat locked down, unable to go out into the snow nor be with my family during that season, I felt the darkness close in on me as if I just wanted to crawl up and die. Thoughts of my mother's passing two months prior and never seeing her on early again made it even worse!

After I dove into my Bible for some answers to remove my head from my buttocks, I found in John 3 all I needed. John 3:30 says, "He must become greater, I must become less." This scripture is John giving testimony about Jesus and is saying when Jesus comes, man must no longer see everything as being about him! This verse seemed to clearly tell me that the darkness I was in was because I made it dark! Once I processed how God sent his son here to die for my selfish self and that I needed to see his blessings as my light that this Christmas would not be as bad as I was about to let the devil make it.

So as I closed out the vision I had meditated on and saw the people gather around the trough with the awful smell in that stable to witness the birth of the hope of the world and celebrate this child born in such a poverty-surrounded environment, I saw nothing but light and true happiness.

I challenge you to make your next Christmas about some strangers you don't even know. What if we changed Christmas and made it Christmasing and took the spirit through the entire year? You ponder on that thought and take action.

ARE YOU IGNORING SIGNS OF MERCY?

*M*Y SLOWNESS TO ACT IS a sign of mercy, not of weakness. When God did not punish the people of Israel quickly, they assumed he lost his power. "He will do nothing! No harm will come to us; we will never see sword of famine" (Jeremiah 5:12). Wow, were they wrong! God had given them a period of probation, but they missed his sign, so when he ran out of options, he resorted to punishment.

What are you doing that you shouldn't be doing that God has sent you a sign to stop and yet you keep doing anyway? Yep, go get a mirror and check yourself and come back and let me break it down for you. Because I will warn you right now before you mark this page and go check yourself and come back. It won't end well if you don't stop!

What I want you to do is process what are you doing that is not pleasing to God and disappointing to him. I want you to write them on a piece of paper. Now beside each one, write down what you can do to please God to replace that thing and then pray on that positive thing. After it's in the universe, make it happen.

When you or if you come to hear me speak, I would like to hear from you when I ask the audience to participate or send me a note at derek@derekgmatthews.com

BREAKING THE SILENCE AFTER YET ANOTHER LOSS

So WHEN I LEFT YOU last, I was working on completing what I believed was the last of my prison stay. Well, as the months grew closer, I would be hit again with even more devastating news that my brother Robert would be found dead in a hotel room. I'm told that after a night of some heavy partying, he did not wake up, and upon the arrival of first responders, he would be pronounced dead on the scene.

So I again must reach deep inside my soul and decide how heavy my reliance on my faith had to be to overcome yet another storm. I began to fast and meditate like never before and ask God to reveal my instructions for the next journey I would find myself entering.

Now you recall, my mother had only passed less than six months prior, so now I must again deal with major devastation. This time, due to a personal request or wishes my brother made while discussing his life during his struggle after my mother became ill, the family would honor his wishes to be cremated, which meant services would be simple and also move fast.

Again I must now wait for arrangements from my family before I can request to attend any services. Now here is where the burden of being in this hellhole gets ugly again. Once I received the date of the arrangements and turn them in, I'm told my counselor is off on some kind of leave and will return in a couple of days. Now time is an issue here because the paperwork must make it to the warden's office and be approved.

After several days of waiting and major running around, I'm told that I will not be allowed to attend any services for my brother. So back to my writing to the warden again. After a week of persistence on my part, I'm granted a twelve-hour furlough to come home and pay respects nine days after my brother had been memorialized. Very upset and even angry, I'm yet very grateful. I'm picked up again by one of my boys, Tim the grumpy old man, we call him. Now with these furloughs, your time begins after they process you out the door, so in order to maximize your time, you start to pray for no traffic and no car troubles. This is also why I'm blessed—I still have a few friends who have badges and guns.

I arrive at my home where I have asked to have at least two hours of private time with my wife before any family shows up. I was clear that I only wanted immediate family come to the house as my time would be very limited.

During this visit, I not only got to sit with family and reflect on our loss, but also process the future as my last few months seemed so far away. After some good home-cooked food, laughter, and prayer, my short furlough would have to come to an end. We would depart my home and head back to federal prison camp that would be my continued residence for another four to five months.

Over the next few months, I remain in my private space deeply rooted in following my faith. My days would remain very structured with reading, exercise, and trying to write out my thoughts.

As the hot summer days came and my time for release grew strong, I worked to narrow my exit plan out as best as I could. I expected my life would be significantly different after processing my journey.

I LOST MY PRAYER

THE MOST VALUABLE RESOURCE WE have is prayer, but as the world feeds us its cruel ways, we seem to dare, yes, dare ourselves to do what's right and use the power of prayer to reach God and live in his sight. As we pray, we learn to set aside our own agendas and cares, set aside our selfish ways and negative thoughts, yes, thoughts with no means, actions with no results, and words with no meaning, and once the prayer is heard, God's priorities become one with ours.

There is no special tongue needed, no education required. Yes, all you need is to be honest, and God will give you the opportunity to have him reveal himself to you. I once lost my prayer and, at one point, didn't even care until I found myself with nothing left and forced my family into an empty nest. Yes, an empty nest with no father, no husband, no guidance, no leadership, because I lost my prayer. I lost my prayer and life took a turn, I lost my prayer and found myself in prison.

WHAT EXACTLY ARE YOU HUNGRY FOR?

WHAT DO I MEAN BY the title of this chapter? As I sat in prison with lots of time to reflect, I began to think how important working out was to us, how important fitness and physical strength was. The more I pondered on the mental game prison played on our minds, the more I began to see how important it was to become a master of my mind, and once I did this, I could master others as well. You see, I found that each of us hungers for different things, and sometimes, those things are the very things that hurt us the most. Let me give you an example of what I mean. Some people hunger for fast food, and while they know it's not healthy, they eat it anyway, and even after getting sick or gaining weight, they continue to eat it anyway. Or take cigarettes, it tells us on the pack that they may cause cancer or even death, but people smoke them all day. It's the same with lust, a man knows he is wrong to be with another woman and yet he does it anyway. I say to you that in order to control your appetites for unpleasant hungers, you must master self-control. The hunger for money can be the root of one's self-destruction, and if you don't control your own self, you will find it to be the root to all your problems in your home and life. I only spoke of a few hungers, but more are or could be. Drugs, profanity, material things, violence, pornography, greed, gossip, sex, gambling, career/job.

What I found as I sat in prison was to block out the things that pertained to me was that I had to convert the emotion attached to things into positive energy to something else. So when I saw something on TV or in a magazine that reminded me of sex, I would redirect that energy into my workout or go look at a picture of my wife and write a letter to express my love to her. Every one of us has an appetite for something that after the pleasure is gone may cause you harm. So yes, if yours is chocolate, then instead of eating that candy bar, go work out or walk.

THE TRUST SHALL SET YOU FREE

*T*HE BIBLE TELLS US IN John 8:31–41, "So if the Son sets you free, you will be free indeed."

The passage hits home with me as I sit in the federal prison as inmate number 820-91-083 feeling like a slave who just wants out of this hell.

As I read the scripture more, I find that Jesus tells the children of Abraham, "I tell you the truth, everyone who sins is a slave to sin. How a slave has no permanent place in the family, but a son belongs to it forever."

As I process this scripture more, I realize that I am only a prisoner by title given by physical captors and that Jesus has already set me free when I admitted to my sins and let go of my sinful ways. At some point, we have to begin to process that we get exactly what we think the most about. The universe is like a magnetic field that directly corresponds to our thoughts and energy.

My example is if you were turning a radio dial trying to find an AM/FM station and the universe was a radio tower that only had AM, what do you think you would hear? (Question)? Yes, nothing! But, if there is an FM tower looking to connect with your choice in FMY tuning, then once you lock it in, you will have whatever you search for. You can't desire to be happy in a relationship and keep giving thought to your bad relationships of the past because the universe will attract those constant negative signals and history will repeat itself. My late great mother, Rev. Callie Matthews, told me years ago that "You will keep getting what you have always gotten if you keep doing what you have always done."

This is why the same 3 percent of the population keep obtaining the wealth while the 97 percent keep working all their lives and never get it. It's because of the difference in how they think.

WHAT FACE DOES YOUR GOD HAVE?

*D*URING MY TIME IN PRISON, I was asked on many occasions by fellow inmates on their spiritual journey what I thought God looked like. I would always reply, "What does he look like to you?" or "Why do you feel God must have a face?"

It was interesting because the black brothers wanted God to be black and others had been led to see white hair, white beard, or their image of Christ was God!

I found that as a result of the questions, my fellow inmates seemed to not take God seriously. Their theories, understandings, and beliefs were unclear at best. People seem to want a god with a face. My Muslim brothers looked to a prophet, my Moore Temple brothers also looked to a prophet (Noble Drew Ali), and of course, Christians and Jews looked to Christ. Conversation after conversation, they would say, "Well, Mr. Matthews, who do you worship?"

I would reply that my mightier power had no face and that when he reveals himself to me, it was a feeling or even a silent voice! They would tell me more! "What its feel?" "What's it sound like?"

One day after I finished a visit with a friend of mine, I was greeted at my bunk by a small group of young men waiting patiently to ask me questions about church service they had just left. The question was regarding the sermon they had just heard where the pastor stated that Jesus showed signs of weakness while on the cross. They were all very upset about this statement and I want to explain. I began by further troubling them by saying, "Guys, Jesus showed lots of weaknesses on the cross."

They were confused and baffled! I asked them to listen close. I began to explain how Jesus wept and even tears of blood. I asked

God why God had forsaken him! I explained to them that God had to at some point turn his back on him so that he would suffer and die in pain because we would live! As I explained how Jesus was forced to carry his own cross while being whipped, stoned, spat on, hit, cursed, and nailed to the cross all for our sins. This was all done so we would never have to carry our own burdens alone. I explained that in our darkest hours, God would take away our pain only if we had faith. The more I spoke, the more my young brothers became sponges for more. I would ask them to consider Jesus Christ! As God is in HD and they would be clarity beyond clarity. I told them they could never go wrong following Christ. From this conversation, they requested more of my time during the week to sit and discuss God and how they could do better in their walks.

TIE UP YOUR LOOSE ENDS

*I*F YOU STOP AND TAKE a few quiet minutes and reflect on the power of God, you would not be able to even speak for a minute. Just say to yourself, "He spoke and the entire universe came to be." Wow, that is just amazing. Now say to yourself, "My life, and thoughts come from him." Okay, you have to feel empowered. The Bible tells us in the book of Genesis that God created earth and he established it upon waters. Now process the fact that God did not create earth and all its treasures to then just leave it, he works night and day to keep it going by nurturing it, because it's his. I thank God for his incredible imagination and allowing me to even be a part of his world.

When I would find myself going off track and feeling negative thoughts coming, I would begin processing Psalm 27.

"The Lord is my light and my salvation; Whom shall I fear? The Lord is the strength of my life; Of whom shall I be afraid? When the wicked came against me To eat up my flesh, My enemies and foes, They stumbled and fell. Though an army may encamp against me, My heart shall not fear; Though war may rise against me, In this I will be confident. One thing I have desired of the Lord, That will I seek: That I may dwell in the house of the Lord All the days of my life, To behold the beauty of the Lord, And to inquire in His temple. For in the time of trouble He shall hide me in His pavilion; In the secret place of his tabernacle He shall hide me; He shall set me high upon a rock. And now my head shall be lifted up above my enemies all around me; Therefore I will offer sacrifices of joy in His tabernacle; I will sing, yes, I will sing praises to the Lord. Hear, O Lord, when I cry with my voice! Have mercy also upon me, and answer me. When You said, 'Seek My face,' My heart said

to You, 'Your face, Lord, I will seek.' Do not hide Your face from me; Do not turn Your servant away in anger; You have been my help; Do not leave me nor forsake me, O God of my salvation. When my father and my mother forsake me, Then the Lord will take care of me. Teach me your way, O Lord, And lead me in a smooth path, because of my enemies. Do not deliver me to the will of my adversaries; For false witnesses have risen against me, And such as breathe out violence. I would have lost heart, unless I had believed that I would see the goodness of the Lord In the land of the living. Wait on the Lord; Be of good courage, And He shall strengthen your heart; Wait, I say, on the Lord!"

This book of the Bible was written by David, the shepherd boy who became Israel's greatest king of all time. Within the 150 psalms are the greatest bunch of prayers ever written. They express grief, depression, anger, love, and joy—all emotions I battled while in prison. I believe that no matter what our emotions are, God wants us to share with him through prayer. God will listen to your concerns and, in his son Jesus's name, answers them. Take a minute to reflect on God's power and let those things of your past go and tie those loose ends once and for all.

IS HIS DOOR OPEN FOR YOU?

$\mathcal{M}$Y MOTHER USED TO ALWAYS say, "Suga, God will forgive us all."

As I sat in federal prison with nothing except time on my hands, I asked myself if God really had an open door policy. As a former big cheese in my career field, we would tell staff, "My door is always open," but if we were busy, angry, or just didn't really care for a person, you might blow a person off if they came to your door. I would sit on occasion and ponder, "I wonder how God works?" As I studied more I came to believe that God's forgiveness to allow an open-door policy must be earned. I mean it's a person-to-person, one-on-one arrangement. In John 14:1, Jesus says, "Do not let your hearts be troubled. Trust in God, trust also in me." He also told the leaders of the Jews, "If anyone keeps my word, he will never see death." There are very clear illustrations used to show Christians that we need to have individual relationships with God in order to have the open door policy when we either need it or we get called to stand before it.

Okay, let me break this down for you a bit more. We are talking about a real personal relationship, one like no other you can speak of. I thought I had one, but after review when sitting in prison, I realized that I had never ever really had a 100 percent committed relationship with not only God, but nothing else or anyone. Wow, that got your attention.

Okay, take a look at this, and before you judge me, go get a mirror and ask yourself:

> Am I committed to my spouse 100 percent?
> Am I committed to my children 100 percent?
> Am I committed to my career/job 100 percent?

Am I committed to my family 100 percent?
Am I committed to myself 100 percent?
Last, now ask yourself, Are you really committed
to God?

If you're committed to your spouse, you love unconditionally and never lust over anyone else (1 Thessalonians). (Write it out.) (Derek, what do you want written out?)

If you're committed to your kids, do you allow work or pleasure to steal time away from them? Do you allow them to feel how important they are to you every day (Psalm 127)?

If you are really committed to your job, do you search the Web during work time for another job? Do you at the last minute call off to pleasure yourself, knowing you are inconveniencing someone else and maybe even their family? Do you treat your boss as if you would want others to treat you if you were the boss?

If you are committed to family, do you love your mother as she loved you as a child and treat her with unconditional love each and every day? (See John 3:3.)

If you are committed to yourself, do you take care of your body with healthy food, exercise, and rest? Do you frequent a doctor on a regular? Do you drink alcohol, smoke, use drugs, or take unnecessary risks that could cause harm or even death?

Now that you have answered all of these questions and sit in shock!

Are you 100 percent committed to God?

This self-evaluation is very hard for all of us due to pride and fear of living in the flesh, but to love and live Christ-like is to humble ourselves and work to answer these very basic questions to the affirmative.

A CLOSE ENCOUNTER

*L*IFE IS FULL OF EXPERIENCES and encounters which provide both challenges to one's character and testing of one's spirit.

To be sure, life is not only composed of experiences and encounters; it also is composed of big questions marks. In every life, there are always questions which ought to be asked and which demand an answer. The first big question of life is always: "Who am I?" And the second question is close to it, and that is "What am I living for?" However, when life has been lived to a level of maturity, when our experiences and encounters have led to some up and downs, some joy and sadness, there is yet another question that most of us asked at some point: "How did I get where I am which seems so far from where I am supposed to be?"

I found that in scripture (1 Kings 19) I see a defeated Elijah sitting under a broom tree in deepest bucket of his own sadness (much like I found myself). In prison, I see an Elijah who had come to a point where he had to ask life's most difficult question: "How did I get to where I am which is so far from where I am supposed to be?"

Okay, let me tell you how I see it! There are only three kinds of people in this world: those who are in the wilderness, those who have just come out of the wilderness, and then those who are headed into the wilderness.

Okay, in scripture right in the midst of that wilderness experience, God sent his angel to feed Elijah, "You don't have enough for your journey!"

He replied, "What journey? I'm through. I'm all washed up."

How many have felt this way?

"You're not through, Elijah." The angel tells him, "I'm going to send you from where you are to where I want you to be. I'm going to send you from the molehill to the mountain, I'm going to send you from the wilderness to the mountain."

In the wilderness, there is weakness, but on the mountain, there is strength. In the wilderness, there is loneliness, but on the mountain, there is companionship. In the wilderness, there is despair, but on the mountain, there is hope.

You may now question, but what is really hope? What we call hoping is only wishing. We want things we think are impossible, but we know better than to spend our money or commit our lives to them.

Biblical hope is an act. Hope acts on the conviction God will complete the work that he has begun even when the appearances, especially when the appearances, oppose it.

So in closing, during your close encounter or wilderness experiences when your character is being tested, let your test be your testimony! Amen!

When you feel as if life itself has hit rock bottom and there is nowhere else to go, you don't need reasons, you need comfort. You don't need some answers; you need someone. And you will find that Jesus doesn't come with explanations, but rather, he comes with his presence.

I found while in federal prison that it seems we are always looking for the reason. We want to know why. "Why did my mother have to die?" or "Why did my brother have to die months after?" "Why am I really in prison?" "Why?" Like Job, we want God to tell us what's going on.

But God does not reveal his plan to us, but instead, he reveals himself. It's clear that he comes when we are down and brings us fellowship. Strength when we are weak, peace when we are troubled, courage when we are afraid, and a loving spouse when we are lonely. He is with us on whatever journey we find ourselves, either at home or in prison. He knows funerals, hospitals, jails, schools, and tears. He knows because he is with us. He comes to be with us over and over again. It's not easy to process or sometimes even easy to begin to believe, but having even only faith the size of a mustard seed is all you need.

I pray this experience has been enlightening and provided you some insight that we can with just a little bit of faith overcome the impossible. Because knowing that nothing is actually impossible to God is half the battle. Since my return to and from my journey, I was faced with many more challenges and road blocks being treated as an African-American male tagged as a felon, and in my next book, I will share what those challenges were and how I also overcame them.

RELEASE MORNING

*A*s I paced the floors all night and packed up my belongings, it was interesting to watch how various people would want your things or some even showed signs of jealousy watching you leave and give personal items away. I had seen many guys go out, but many more come in and today was my day to go out, and that's all that mattered to me.

You sit on your bunk until you're called by the on-duty CO to be escorted over to processing. When my call would come, it would be yet another yet interesting exchange between a CO that I could not stand! This guy had it in for me because he just could not figure me out. He struggled with how I could interact with every circle/group in the prison and received more respect than most COs got. When he got the call to send me over, he would fix his mouth to not only call my name, but he had a vicious remark for me by saying, "You're not going home, you're being sent somewhere else," and he just laughed as if his joke was so funny. Then as I walked out with several other inmates assisting in carrying my belongings, he said, "See you when you get back."

Well, as much as this pissed me off, I refused to let him know it and said, "God bless you."

The walk across the yard was a bit interesting. I can see where cars waiting to pick people up are located, but I don't see any for me. I began to get anxious because they may not release you that day if you miss your time window. Now as the guys walk with me, I see an unmarked SUV, and as we all look that direction, it turned its emergency lights on and it lit up like a Christmas tree. Yes, it was that damn Vince and Tim! Vince has come to get me in his work vehicle.

Of course, I had never made a public announcement I was a former law enforcement officer, but well aware everyone knew it. Oh well, I'm going home now, so who cares, right?

IS THIS ENDING OR JUST STARTING?

So as I close out my journey through this temporary hell and look to my new life back in the world, it's now you will see where my faith will really be challenged.

For a solid year, I had heard my guys talk about refusing to leave prison to avoid going to a halfway house and I could not understand this at all. Now stay with me here. I'm being released in two weeks and my wife reveals to me she may have breast cancer. I ask myself, "What the hell is next?"

As I listen to her voice, I can actually feel her fear through the recorded line inside the prison phone room. It became hard to pray, for it was so overwhelming to clear my mind to even concentrate. She would begin her initial appointments as I now complete my final days in federal prison.

I'M OUT OF HERE

GET PROCESSED OUT AND WATCHED several inmates get picked up by other agencies, and I'm just praying to walk out the door. As I enter the vehicle after lots of hugs and kisses, I can smell fried chicken wings!

They give you just enough time to make it to your destination. So shy of breaking any traffic laws, we drive and make good time. I arrive at the halfway house in Baltimore City and begin a process that just seems like another money machine for the government. Conditions subpar, staff unprofessional, and yet it's part of the process. I'm told by staff that for the first seven days, you can't leave the facility for any reason. You're forced to take a series of classes that the staff barely shows up to even teach.

After you take the classes, you are fitted with an ankle monitor. Yes, in a week, I too would be wearing an ankle monitor! Who would ever thought this too would become a part of life's journey.

Now let's not forget I'm now processed into this new environment that's subpar to where I had been housed for the past year, and on top of it all, my wife had breast cancer standing at her front door. While I have dealt with great sacrifice through this past eighteen months, nothing compares to my feelings of my wife having something that took my mother away such a short time ago. And the system would have my seven days turned into fourteen before I could be authorized to start leaving to go to work and attend church on Sundays. I would have to play this game for forty-five days while working at a local law firm for less than $10 per hour and I would have to give 25 percent of that pay to fund the halfway house for monitoring fees. Sounds criminal, right?

PROBATION OFFICER

ES, IT HAD BEEN ORDERED that I have supervised probation for one year after my release. Now this was interesting because while these folks are not in their jobs to be your friends, I could tell mine knew that I was not the everyday felon, and I believe we kept a level of respect for each other that worked well for the both of us. I was also ordered to pay back the $12,000 I was paid for the consulting agreement and the clock was ticking. Oh, did I mention that I was served papers while in prison that stated I would be banned from any government contract work, small business loans, and no major companies would be able to use my resume as their person for five years.

Now this had the smell and taste of being very personal since the original time line for others was two years, but they amended the time frame for me citing that due to my position and influence the United States government had to protect itself from me.

MY BRIDE DIGS IN FOR THE FIGHT

ARLA WOULD RECEIVE HER SURGERY date, and we would now prepare ourselves for her fight. Early September after many appointments, consults, and lab work, my wife would report to the hospital for breast cancer surgery. The surgery would be for fourteen long hours. I believe the world stopped for fourteen hours as I waited in that waiting room, not leaving even for a second.

It was like for fourteen hours, my life depended on the outcome of what happened in that operating room. When the doctors and the plastic surgeon came out with good news, my heart started to beat again. Her road to recovery would be good because she was a fighter.

PUTTING PLANS INTO ACTION

WHILE AWAY, I HAD DECIDED that once I was cleared to have my own business, I would open a self-defense/boxing fitness location. So I did just that. I launched a small local establishment that catered to women and people with a goal to want to defend themselves during times of personal attack. My social media campaign and name within the community gave me some good face time with community leaders, but business proved to be very competitive and after one year became an uphill fight trying to secure desired funding to grow. Yes, the scarlet letter of being a felon is real, and the ban placed on me not allowing me access to my former world stung like a bee.

OPTIONS ON THE TABLE

*D*URING THIS STRUGGLING TIME AND having met many, many people, I was approached by a group with an idea to eradicate homelessness in the inner cities. I met a businessman in the marketing field that had an idea I truly bought into, and after some negotiation, we made an agreement. He would cover my studio expenses and allow my life story to be featured in my own publication and that he would basically finance while I did the ground work.

The arrangement began with lots of excitement, but after a few months, I also had many unanswered questions on the solid direction of the project. After three to four months of butting heads turning into heated discussions, I decided it was best to part ways and disconnect from the businessman and the project.

ONE DOOR CLOSES AND A WINDOW OPENS

*N*OW DURING THE TIME OF running my business, I caught the eye of local government. So it is here that things get crazy again. I accept a job with my city's housing authority after being vetted by the federal agency that had oversight over the City's Housing Authority; knowing my full history, they hired me with clear direction that I had nothing to be concerned about because the process had cleared me. I dove into this position with 100 percent energy, working hard, setting up community meetings, and working with the local police. It was only after two solid weeks on the job that my local newspaper fielded some questions by a small makeup of bitter community people with too much time on their hands who believed I didn't deserve a second chance. So after a news article comes out, "Does He Deserve a Second Chance" after several days of media interaction, I was terminated without cause.

This termination would mean I had used the last of my savings to open a business that I placed on hold and now stood losing, after agreeing to not have that business be a conflict while on the job.

You can imagine my disappointment after such hard work to be told you didn't deserve a second chance after enduring the pain I had endured for such a small infraction. I would ask myself again, "When would it end?"

Well, didn't buy that for too long. I hired a few lawyers to assist me in handling paying the publication debt back and handle the lease issue from the self-defense studio. I would find some basic work at a local car rental place who after hearing my story allowed me a part-time job to earn a living.

It's here where I would re-humble myself and plan my next strategic move. After a few months of prayer, faith building, and lots of sleepless nights, I would be approached to oversee a project in Africa for six to nine months.

I truly believe that God makes no mistakes and sending me oversees was another avenue to greatness. While overseas opportunities for new growth continue as my faith continues to get me through.

ABOUT THE AUTHOR

Born and raised in Annapolis, Maryland, Derek G. Matthews has been married for twenty-five years to the love of his love and is a father of twins who are both in their senior year of college. Mr. Matthews is an astute businessman who has extensive international travel providing his expertise in many countries around the world. He is a solid leader in the community and through the United Methodist Church serving as a certified lay speaker having aspirations of being a pastor, following his mother and grandfather. He has served as active member of the AA County NAACP where he has held positions to include chair of economic development. He also very active in the Prince Hall Masons Rising Sun Lodge 46 in Arnold, Maryland. Derek has had a diverse senior level law enforcement career serving local and federal government level agencies as well as the private sector. Mr. Matthews has served his country well in many prominent positions which include senior government official, Prince Georges County Sheriff's office and assistant police chief in the City of Glenarden, Maryland. He is an internationally sought-after speaker for keynote addresses, corporate motivational seminars for corporations, organizations, groups, and churches.

He has made solid contributions in law enforcement across the nation to include training and security management, quality assurance programs, and officer survival programs for local law enforcement agencies at the local, state, and federal levels. What he prides himself on the most is being a man of solid faith who loves his family and believes God has allowed him to overcome many obstacles because of his faith.

CPSIA information can be obtained
at www.ICGtesting.com
Printed in the USA
LVHW040539210820
663704LV00003B/144

9 781635 687279